The excellence of every art must consist in the complete accomplishment of its purpose.

A Persistence of Vision

Arnold Schwartzman

For Steve.
With my fondest
best wishes.

Arnold Schwartzman
2005

images
Publishing

First published in Australia in 2005 by
The Images Publishing Group Pty Ltd
ABN 89 059 734 431
6 Bastow Place, Mulgrave, Victoria, 3170, Australia
Telephone: +61 3 9561 5544
Facsimile: +61 3 9561 4860
books@images.com.au
www.imagespublishing.com

Schwartzman, Arnold
A Persistence of Vision:
Arnold Schwartzman profiles his work
in Graphic Design and Film
ISBN 1 86470 121 8.

Design: Arnold Schwartzman
Digital artwork: Isolde Schwartzman
Printed by: Paramount Printing Co Ltd Hong Kong

IMAGES has included on its website a page for
special notices in relation to this and its other
publications.
Please visit: www.imagespublishing.com

Every effort has been made to trace the original
source of copyright material contained in this
book. The publishers would be pleased to hear
from copyright holders to rectify any errors or
omissions. The information and illustrations in this
publication have been prepared and supplied by
Arnold Schwartzman. While all reasonable efforts
have been made to ensure accuracy, the publishers
do not, under any circumstances, accept responsi-
bility for errors, omissions and representations
expressed or implied.

Frontispiece photograph: Cornel Lucas
Endpapers: Arnold Schwartzman's
fingerprints, U.S. Immigration and
Naturalization Service.

Dedicated to my wife and partner, Isolde,

and to my friends and mentors:
Abram Games (1914 – 1996)
Saul Bass (1920 – 1996)

Contents

Introduction   6

1950s   11

1960s   14

1970s/1980s   38

1990s   72

2000+   108

Profile   127

Timeline of American Jewish history. One of six 10-foot-high permanent exhibition panels for the Skirball Cultural Center, Los Angeles.

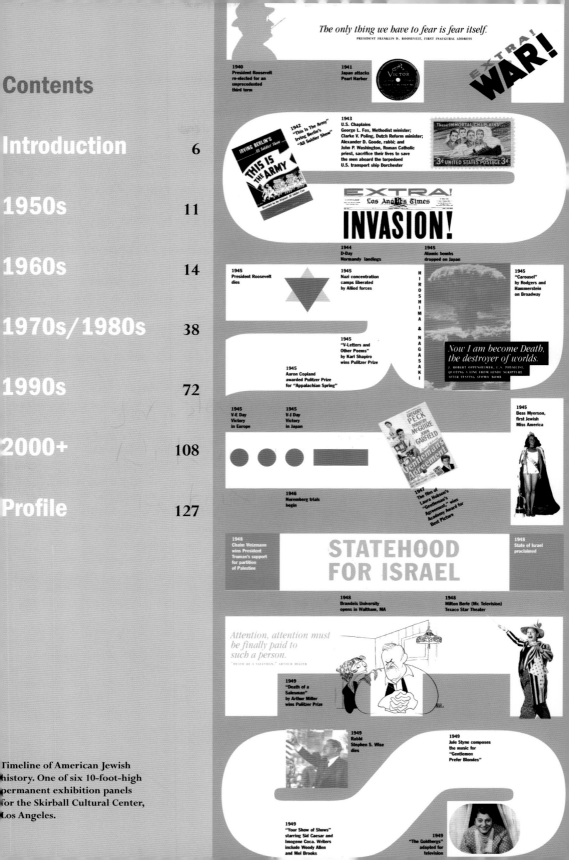

The only thing we have to fear is fear itself.
PRESIDENT FRANKLIN D. ROOSEVELT, FIRST INAUGURAL ADDRESS

1940
President Roosevelt re-elected for an unprecedented third term

1941
Japan attacks Pearl Harbor

EXTRA! WAR!

1942
"This Is The Army" Irving Berlin's "All Soldier Show"

1943
U.S. Chaplains
George L. Fox, Methodist minister; Clarke V. Poling, Dutch Reform minister; Alexander D. Goode, rabbi; and John P. Washington, Roman Catholic priest, sacrifice their lives to save the men aboard the torpedoed U.S. transport ship Dorchester

These IMMORTAL CHAPLAINS
3¢ UNITED STATES POSTAGE 3¢

EXTRA!
Los Angeles Times
INVASION!

1944
D-Day
Normandy landings

1945
Atomic bombs dropped on Japan

1945
President Roosevelt dies

1945
Nazi concentration camps liberated by Allied forces

HIROSHIMA & NAGASAKI

1945
"Carousel" by Rodgers and Hammerstein on Broadway

1945
"V-Letters and Other Poems" by Karl Shapiro wins Pulitzer Prize

Now I am become Death, the destroyer of worlds.
J. ROBERT OPPENHEIMER, U.S. PHYSICIST, QUOTING A LINE FROM HINDU SCRIPTURE AFTER TESTING ATOMIC BOMB

1945
Aaron Copland awarded Pulitzer Prize for "Appalachian Spring"

1945
V-E Day
Victory in Europe

1945
V-J Day
Victory in Japan

GREGORY PECK
DOROTHY McGUIRE
JOHN GARFIELD
Gentleman's Agreement

1945
Bess Myerson, first Jewish Miss America

1946
Nuremberg trials begin

1947
The film of Laura Hobson's "Gentleman's Agreement," wins Academy Award for Best Picture

1948
Chaim Weizmann wins President Truman's support for partition of Palestine

STATEHOOD FOR ISRAEL

1948
State of Israel proclaimed

1948
Brandeis University opens in Waltham, MA

1948
Milton Berle (Mr. Television) Texaco Star Theater

Attention, attention must be finally paid to such a person.
"DEATH OF A SALESMAN," ARTHUR MILLER

1949
"Death of a Salesman" by Arthur Miller wins Pulitzer Prize

1949
Rabbi Stephen S. Wise dies

1949
Jule Styne composes the music for "Gentlemen Prefer Blondes"

1949
"Your Show of Shows" starring Sid Caesar and Imogene Coca. Writers include Woody Allen and Mel Brooks

1949
"The Goldbergs" adapted for television

What do graphic designers do when they reach 60? was the question posed to me by the General Manager of the television network where I worked as a twenty-something graphic designer. Due to be promoted to a senior position, I responded, without hesitation: *They become better designers, sir!* Now that I am well past that milestone I like to think I gave the correct answer.

I was born in a former Victorian workhouse, just a stone's throw from London's Tower Bridge, where a century ago my grandparents arrived after escaping the pogroms of Eastern Europe. At age four I survived a direct hit by an incendiary bomb on our home on the first day of the Blitz. Following my evacuation to the countryside, I was placed in the village school with much older children, where the teacher, not having much time to spend with me, plied me with cigarette cards and foreign postage stamps to keep me occupied. Not able to read, I entertained myself at home by looking at magazines such as *Life* and *Saturday Evening Post*, which my father received from American servicemen who frequented the Savoy Hotel where he worked as a waiter. Although Hitler's bombs disrupted my formal education, I was compensated by the introduction to a visual world. This was in part due to the small monthly magazine *Lilliput*, which pioneered the concept of interspersing picture comparisons between short articles, e.g. a top-hatted cleric opposite a similar-hatted German chimney sweep.

By age nine I was finally able to read. Prior to my discovery of Aldus Manutius, my interest in the printed word was spelling out my name on those ubiquitous cast-iron stamping machines found on British Railway platforms. My frustration was that for my penny's worth the metal strip could not accommodate the number of characters in my long name.

At the end of WWII, my parents opened a small hotel, the Majestic, in Cliftonville on England's southeast coast. For my ninth birthday, they gave me a 9.5 mm Pathé hand-cranked film projector which initiated my passion for motion pictures. Two years later I was captivated to see a film being shot on the beach in front of the hotel. The film's director, observing my interest in the production, invited me to be an extra.

During my school holidays, a friend of my parents, the owner of a local cinema, asked if I would like to work as an assistant projectionist. After just one day on the job I decided I would rather be behind a camera than a projector!

There's a good future in plastics. The following school break, another family acquaintance gave me a job in his plastics factory. The job entailed stencilling floral designs onto plastic cups. Apart from the toxic fumes, the task didn't exactly tax my artistic aspirations.

During the summer, armed with pencil and pad and a series of *How To Draw* books, I would go down to the local park on Sundays to watch the cricket while diligently copying the examples from the books.

Often sitting behind me on the grass were the two comedians who were appearing at the local seaside variety show – the then unknown Reg Varney and his straight-man Benny Hill. Glancing over my shoulder, Hill once quipped: *Your noses are coming along very nicely!*

Arnold, age 2.

6

Two guests who stayed at the Majestic played an important part in shaping my future career. One was caricaturist Ralph Sallon, who was visiting the town to attend a political party conference that he was covering for his newspaper. Aware of my interest in drawing, he took me along, and sat me beside him in the wings of the Winter Gardens theatre where I watched him sketch Britain's leading politicians. It was sheer magic to see the artist's work printed in the next morning's daily newspaper.

The other visitor who made a great impression on me was Abram Games, the leading graphic designer who had just designed the symbol for the 1951 Festival of Britain. Games became a friend and mentor, whose design philosophy has remained a source of inspiration throughout my career.

That same year, I enrolled at the local art school. However, my future in design almost ended before it started. Being a keen weightlifter and body builder, I was caught one day by the school's principal lifting two heavy book-binding presses above my head, which resulted in a serious discussion forcing me to decide on which vocation to follow.

Life is full of making decisions – in retrospect I made the right one. But, who knows, if I had opted for the alternative – I might have ended up as Governor of California!

After completing an intermediate course, I moved on to Canterbury College of Art,

Schwartzman's first printed design: linocut of a "font of type" for the typeface catalogue cover, Canterbury College of Art, 1954.

where I graduated with the Ministry of Education's National Diploma in Design.

For the next couple of years I became 23179534 Private Schwartzman. As a National Serviceman my first "professional" assignment was on board a troopship during the several weeks' voyage to Korea.

Designated an "artist", I was given the task of retouching the ship's name *R.M.S. Empire Orwell* on her life belts. Aspiring to be a perfectionist and wishing to display my recently acquired skills, I decided not just to retouch the existing lettering, but to recreate the ship's name in red on a fresh coat of white paint.

After weeks of my painstaking work, the ship's boatswain came to inspect my efforts and was shocked to discover what I had done. He explained that the weight of the additional layer of lead paint rendered them useless, and that the several hundred life belts now would fail the Ministry of Trade's buoyancy test!

Whilst in Korea, I was given several artistic tasks. One was to paint a mural in our company's mess hall. Like Michelangelo in the Sistine Chapel, I took my time over it, as I was excused duties and given my own accommodation at the back of the Quonset hut.

Late one Sunday morning I was awakened by loud knocking on the door. To my horror it was our Commanding Officer, who wished to show off my handiwork to a visiting Australian

7

Army chief. With no time to get dressed, still in my pyjamas and wrapped up to my waist in my sleeping bag, I hopped kangaroo-like alongside the two officers as they surveyed my artistic creation.

An article published in the *Journal of the Royal Army Chaplains' Department* described my involvement in fabricating the memorial to the British regiment, the Glorious Glosters:

By July, Korea is in the midst of a season

My efforts were rewarded with a special regimental tie presented to me by our Commanding Officer, who said: *If in your future career you do not produce anything of great significance you can look back on this achievement with pride.* About to exit the orderly room, I was stopped by an officer: *That'll be 10/6d for the tie, Schwartzman –* more than half my week's wages!

Recently I obtained a copy of my service

"Picture comparison", a spread from *Lilliput*, 1941.

of heavy and almost continuous rain. It was impossible to have the ceremony any later than June 29, but it proved impossible to get the slabs from Hong Kong by that date. An artist, Private Schwartzman, of the Royal Sussex Regiment, painted plywood imitation slabs as temporary makeshifts to enable the ceremony to take place. So cleverly was the work executed with due regard to the angle of the sun and the positioning of the shadows, that many people had to be convinced that they were imitations.

report, in which my C.O. wrote:

Military conduct: Very Good. This soldier has shown himself to be reliable and well-behaved. His standard of intelligence places him above his comrades. He is a good artist and can carry out all sign-writing tasks.

He is completely honest and trustworthy, reasonably tidy and smart. His hobby is cine photography, and he could be employed as a unit photographer.

On returning to civvy street I was eventually hired as the sole graphic designer for a local television station in Southampton. This was in the days of black and white television and before video recording.

The job required providing screeds of lettering, which allowed me little time to exercise my creative prowess.

In spite of the C.O.'s praise I wasn't too skilled at hand-lettering and the only system available to me at that time for producing titles was the new Letraset transfer system.

of very talented designers I was spurred on to produce better work.

Ever ambitious, after seven years at the network, I decided to pay a visit to New York, where at that time so much innovative work was being created. I got to meet many of my design heroes. One of them, Lou Dorfsman, the creative director of CBS Television, insisted that I stay and work for him there and then, which I did for the remaining several weeks

Arnold, Stamford Hill, London, 1941.

Arnold, Buckingham Palace, London, 2002.

I had to cut out each individual letter with a scalpel, wet the reverse side and place it onto a cotton screen, then transfer it on to the artwork, in some instances a roller caption. As the letters passed over the machine's rollers, some of the characters would pop off, which required me to stand by in the studio during the live transmissions and quickly replace the missing letters!

After approximately a year I moved on to a design post at Associated-Rediffusion Television, London. Working alongside a group

of my stay in the United States.

On my return to London, I found two positive responses to my recent job applications: one, from Doyle Dane Bernbach in New York, (*Len Sirowitz and I looked at your reel together. We think it's exceptionally good. He also praised your graphics... Ben Spiegel, V.P., DDB*) and from another advertising agency, Erwin Wasey Ltd, London, for a senior creative position, which resulted in several fruitful years as their concept planning executive. I worked on a number of blue-chip accounts including Philips Electrical and Coca-Cola.

In 1969 I was offered a directorship on the Board of the Conran Design Group by Terence Conran, the successful design entrepreneur. Unfortunately I soon realised that leading a large group of designers was not my forte, and that I functioned much better on my own.

For the next several years I divided my time as a designer, illustrator, magazine editor, art gallery director, and for a period, I worked as a somewhat undistinguished television commercials director.

Around this time, I was asked by a friend, the owner of a well-known restaurant club, to collaborate on producing a celebrity cook-book for a charity. One of the designers that I persuaded to contribute an illustration was the celebrated American designer and film maker Saul Bass.

Some five years later, when Saul invited me to become his Design Director in Los Angeles, he was quoted in the press as saying that "this was possibly a marriage made in heaven". After only half a year I once again came to the conclusion that I perform better as an individual.

On Saul's recommendation to the Simon Wiesenthal Center (*Mr. Bass tells us you're a genius.*) I was commissioned to make *Genocide*, a documentary film on the subject of the Holocaust. Thus began my working partnership with my wife Isolde – a true "marriage made in heaven".

Elizabeth Taylor, sitting down opposite me in her suite at the Savoy Hotel, London, had just mixed me a perfect Bloody Mary. The screen legend then began to read quietly to me from the *Genocide* script. For a moment, my mind drifted back to the days when my father beguiled me with his stories of the Hollywood stars he had served in this very hotel. As my gaze wandered out of the window

down to the ancient Thames-side obelisk of Cleopatra, the irony did not escape me that here I was in the presence of Hollywood's incarnation of the Queen of the Nile.

Two and a half years later, at the 1982 Academy Awards, screenwriter Colin Welland, prompted by the evening's previous British wins by Sir John Gielgud and myself, proclaimed in his acceptance speech, *The British are coming!*

That same year I was appointed the Director of Design for the 1984 Los Angeles Olympic Games, which afforded me the opportunity to connect with Los Angeles' design community. A number of books and films followed. For a documentary on the Savoy Hotel, I hired Ralph Sallon to portray some of the personalities featured in my film.

In 1994 I had the pleasure of putting on an exhibition of Abram Games' posters. His inscription to me in the catalogue reads: *For Arnold S, whom I critiqued so heavily when he first visited me as a student and has survived that drilling so nobly and with credit, Abram.*

Over the years I have undertaken a number of extramural roles, including Chairman, and now a Governor, of the British Academy of Film and Television Arts/Los Angeles. During my tenure as Chair of the Documentary Executive Committee of the Academy of Motion Picture Arts and Sciences, I was instrumental in establishing the Documentary Branch of the Academy.

These past 45 years I have zig-zagged through a number of opportunities and challenges, most of which I have relished to the fullest and now feel I am just catching my second wind. Those halcyon days of the Swinging 60s and Lennon & McCartney's lyrics still resonate: *Will you still need me, will you still feed me. When I'm sixty-four? –* or more?

— ARNOLD SCHWARTZMAN, HOLLYWOOD, 2005

1950
"Clarinet Concerto"
by Aaron Copland
premiered by
Benny Goodman

1950
"South Pacific" by
Richard Rodgers,
Oscar Hammerstein
and Joshua Logan,
wins Pulitzer Prize

*...I cannot and will not
cut my conscience to
fit this year's fashions.*
LILLIAN HELLMAN

1950
Korean War
U.S. backs
South Korea
against
the North

1950
Color television first
introduced in U.S.

1951
Lillian Hellman subpoenaed
to appear before the House
Un-American Activities Committee

1951
"The Catcher
in the Rye" by
J. D. Salinger

"I LIKE IKE"

1952
Dwight D. Eisenhower
elected President

1952
Felix Bloch
awarded the
Nobel Prize
in physics

1952
"Caine Mutiny" by
Herman Wouk
wins Pulitzer Prize

In spite of everything I still believe that people are really good at heart...
FROM THE DIARY OF ANNE FRANK

1952
"Anne Frank:
The Diary of a
Young Girl"
appears in English
translation from
the Dutch

1953
"The Crucible"
by Arthur Miller

1954
Jonas Salk develops
the first effective
anti-polio vaccine

'...Could you patent the sun?'
JONAS SALK, WHEN ASKED WHO OWNED THE POLIO VACCINE PATENT

1955
Disc jockey
Alan Freed
coins the phrase
"rock 'n' roll"

"ROCK 'N' ROLL"

1955
Physicist
Albert Einstein
dies

1956
A call for
nuclear
disarmament

$$E=mc^2$$

1956
Hank Greenberg
elected to Baseball
Hall of Fame

1957
Desegregation,
Little Rock, AR

1958
"Night" by
Elie Wiesel

1958
Solomon R. Guggenheim
Museum opens

1956
"My Fair Lady," by
Alan Jay Lerner and
Frederick Loewe,
opens on
Broadway

1959
"Act One"
by Moss Hart
opens on
Broadway

THIS PAGE AND OPPOSITE:
Programme promotion slides
for Granada TV, Southern
Television, and Associated-
Rediffusion Television.

SMS

Somerset Maugham Stories

THE ALIEN CORN

... A generation of young directors and artists is changing the pattern of television, they are helping to emerge from the cramping influence of the theatre proscenium arch... giving it all the fluidity and versatility that the camera allows, in a word – televisual... Schwartzman, in a job he has largely invented, are among them.

— TELE FELLOW, PROFILE ON ARNOLD SCHWARTZMAN, *THE SUNDAY TIMES*, OCTOBER 21, 1965.

1960
"Exodus," directed by Otto Preminger, based on the book by Leon Uris

EXODUS

1961
"West Side Story," by Leonard Bernstein, lyrics by Stephen Sondheim, wins Academy Award for Best Picture

WEST SIDE STORY

1961
Bay of Pigs invasion

1962
Cuban missile crisis

1963
President Kennedy assassinated in Dallas, TX

...that we shall pay any price, bear any burden, meet any hardship... to assure the survival and the success of liberty.

PRESIDENT JOHN F. KENNEDY, INAUGURAL ADDRESS

PREMIERE EDITION — Los Angeles Times — EXTRA — RACE RESULTS

KENNEDY DEAD
Assassin Flees After Shooting

1963
More than 2,000 Kosher products manufactured

1963
"The Feminine Mystique" by Betty Friedan

(K)

1964
F.B.I. find bodies of civil rights workers James Chaney, Andrew Goodman and Michael Schwerner

1964
"Fiddler on the Roof" music by Jerry Bock, lyrics by Sheldon Harnick

1964
U.S. enters Vietnam war

1965
Watts riots, Los Angeles

MALC x LM

SIX DAY WAR

...I felt my legs were praying.

ABRAHAM JOSHUA HESCHEL, ON MARCHING WITH MARTIN LUTHER KING JR., FROM SELMA TO MONTGOMERY, AL, 1965

1965 Malcolm X assassinated . . . .

1965
Felix Frankfurter, Supreme Court Justice, dies

1966
"The Fixer" by Bernard Malamud wins Pulitzer Prize

לֹא תַעֲמֹד עַל-דַּם רֵעֶךָ
"THOU SHALT NOT STAND IDLY BY."

1967
Egypt and Syria agree to U.N. cease-fire as Israeli troops reach Suez Canal

1967
Architect Moshe Safdie designs Habitat for Expo 67, Montreal

1968
The Reverend Martin Luther King Jr. slain in Memphis, TN

1968
Student revolt led by Mark Rudd at Columbia University

...I have seen the promised land.

THE REV. MARTIN LUTHER KING JR.

ACROSS
10 Roth's malady

DOWN
5 Chaim, to Potok

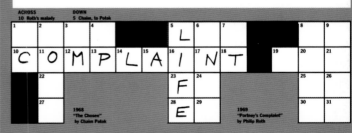

COMPLAINT

LIFE

1968
"The Chosen" by Chaim Potok

1969
"Portnoy's Complaint" by Philip Roth

1969
400,000 attend Woodstock

3 DAYS of PEACE & MUSIC

That's one small step for man, one giant leap for mankind.

NEIL ARMSTRONG

1969
American astronauts Col. Edwin E. Aldrin Jr. and Neil A. Armstrong, first men on the moon

ABOVE: Four of a series of illustrations for a television gala programme which included Prokofiev's *Peter and the Wolf*, narrated by Richard Attenborough, Associated-Rediffusion Television, 1960.

OPPOSITE: A frame from an animated film for a children's programme, Associated-Rediffusion Television.

There were some delightful things of yours in Gebrauchsgraphik, which made me want to see more of your work...

— LETTER FROM TOM WOLSEY, ART DIRECTOR, *MAN ABOUT TOWN*, 1960.

I'd just like to thank you for the magnificent animated titles you did for An ABC of Democracy yesterday. I have had lots of favourable comments on them and am extremely grateful to you for your work.

— MEMO FROM THE HEAD OF FEATURES, *ASSOCIATED-REDIFFUSION TELEVISION*, 1962.

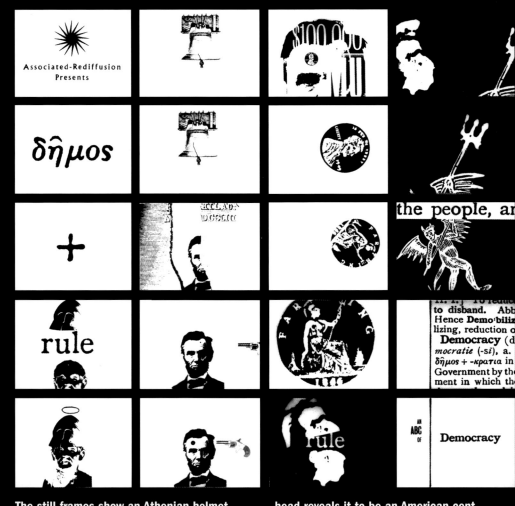

The still frames show an Athenian helmet dissolve into the Liberty Bell, the emergence of Lincoln's head through the crack in the bell, his assassination and the gradual transformation of his head into the reward notice.

Moving into the bullet hole in Lincoln's head reveals it to be an American cent, which dissolves into an English farthing, and Britannia's trident becomes a devil's pitchfork, and finally, the devil's elimination by the emergence of the word "Democracy" in the *Oxford English Dictionary.*

CRIME AND PUNISHMENT

Frames from the opening title
sequence for the television
drama programme, Dostoyevsky's
Crime and Punishment.
Photographs: Donald McCullin.

THIS PAGE AND OPPOSITE:
Programme promotion slides,
Associated–Rediffusion
Television.

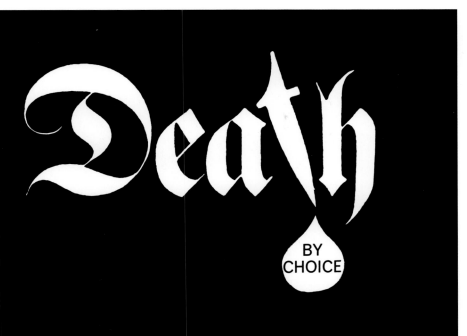

22

THIS PAGE AND OPPOSITE:
Cover designs for *Fusion*,
Associated-Rediffusion
Television's house magazine.

HOUSE MAGAZINE OF REDIFFUSION LONDON AUTUMN

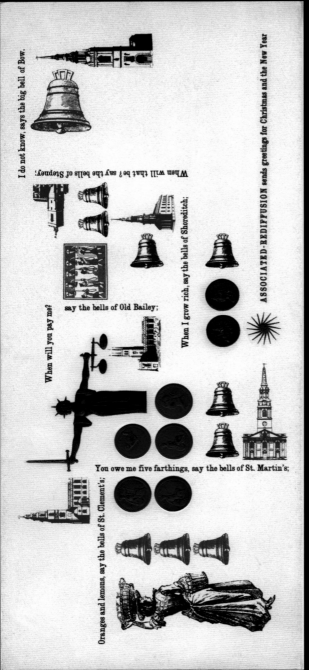

Christmas card,
Oranges and Lemons, for
Associated-Rediffusion Television.
The network's headquarters was
located in the ancient parish of
St. Clement Danes, where the
children's rhyme originated.

OPPOSITE:
1: Symbol for German Undergrou[nd]
Hospital Museum, Jersey,
Channel Islands.
2: A "fool's cap" and the initials
C and P become the logo for
Creative Partners, a team of
comedy script writers.
3: A closed and open camera
iris fabricated in brass forms the
symbol for the set of the weekly
current affairs programme,
This Week, Associated-Rediffusion
Television.
4: Symbol for *Ready, Steady, Go!*
The word "Go" transforms into
a record groove.

1

2

25

3

4

The Beatles in rehearsal for *Ready, Steady, Go!*. On Friday nights, Schwartzman enjoyed taking his camera down to the studio and photographing the various performers appearing on the show.

working in television in London's "Swinging 60s" was an exciting time.

One of the shows, *Ready, Steady, Go!*, seemed to capture the spirit of the period more than any other. About every six weeks, I would produce a new opening title sequence to the programme, cut to the latest hit record.

One day, Andrew Oldham, the Rolling Stones' manager, came to me with a large demo disc, offering the recording for my consideration. I told Andrew that it was great, and if only he could produce a shorter version, the track would be perfect for our needs.

This single – *Satisfaction* – an instant success, became one of the great icons of rock music.

I wish I knew whatever happened to my original disc!

Programme host Cathy McGowan and Schwartzman on the set of *Ready, Steady, Go!*

Ready, Steady, Go! programme host Cathy McGowan is featured in this fast-cutting opening title sequence containing veiled sexual images (cuts less than four frames were seen to be subliminal and not permitted by the censor).

Frames from the opening title sequence for *Ready, Steady, Go!* featuring The Who's track *My Generation*. This was filmed at Wembley Stadium with a group of students from the Royal College of Art who were versed in the art of skateboarding, a fad recently imported from the United States. Associated–Rediffusion Television.

31

A tambourine decorated for
The Byrds' appearance on
Ready, Steady, Go!.
Associated-Rediffusion
Television.

Illustration for an article relating
to the Russian Revolution for
New Society magazine, 1965.

I think your first drawing is one of the best to appear in **New Society** *for a very long time.*

— ROGER PROTZ, ART EDITOR, *NEW SOCIETY*, 1965.

Illustrations for

Arnold Schwartzman

My illustration for *Queen* was also featured in a live TV commercial for the magazine. The next day, I received a telephone call from the publisher, who was greatly concerned as the Camp Coffee company was considering legal action for alleged plagiarism of its label.

"Myth", a collage illustrating an article on the British Raj

magazine's Christmas issue.
Art director: Tom Wolsey.

things go
better
with
Coke
TRADE MARK REG.

1969

May

S	M	T	W	T	F	S
				1	2	3
4	5	6	7	8	9	10
11	12	13	14	15	16	17
18	19	20	21	22	23	24
25	26	27	28	29	30	31

June

S	M	T	W	T	F	S
1	2	3	4	5	6	7
8	9	10	11	12	13	14
15	16	17	18	19	20	21
22	23	24	25	26	27	28
29	30					

OPPOSITE: "Media's Magic
Moments", a promotion kit on
the history of communication
for the *New TV Times*.
Erwin Wasey Ltd Advertising.

D&AD Silver Award for
Outstanding Direct Mail, 1969.

ABOVE: Calendar page for
The Coca-Cola Company.
Photographs: Clive Arrowsm
Erwin Wasey Ltd Advertising

Arnold Schwartzman is 36, and so far has done the work of four lifetimes. His career in design and the graphic arts is phenomenal... phenomenal not only as a success story, but because of the influence he has in our everyday life. He unwittingly educates us to see. Each period has its style and a way of making attractive. We buy the record sleeve as much as the record, read the copy because of the startling illustration. Where there's an image, there's a Schwartzman.

— *THE IMAGE* ARTS MAGAZINE, 1972.

38

The frontiers of photo-graphics were extended by Kieser, Rambo, Lienemeyer and Grindler in Germany, Nakamura in Japan, Dubois in France, Milani in Italy, and Wolf and Schwartzman in the U.S.A.

— F.H.K. HENRION, THE 70s SUMMARY, *AGI ANNALS*, 1989.

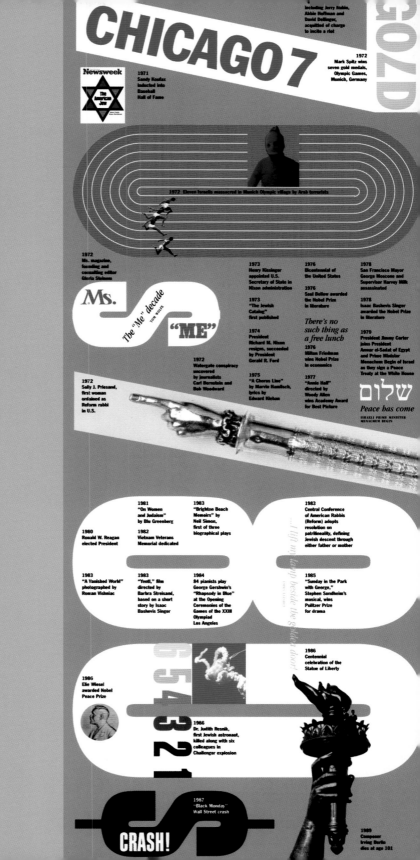

CHICAGO 7

including Jerry Rubin, Abbie Hoffman and David Dellinger, acquitted of charge to incite a riot

1972
Mark Spitz wins seven gold medals, Olympic Games, Munich, Germany

Newsweek
The American Jew

1971
Sandy Koufax inducted into Baseball Hall of Fame

1972 Eleven Israelis massacred in Munich Olympic village by Arab terrorists

1972
Ms. magazine, founding and consulting editor Gloria Steinem

Ms.

The "Me" decade
TOM WOLFE

"ME"

1972
Sally J. Priesand, first woman ordained as Reform rabbi in U.S.

1972
Watergate conspiracy uncovered by journalists Carl Bernstein and Bob Woodward

1973
Henry Kissinger appointed U.S. Secretary of State in Nixon administration

1973
"The Jewish Catalog," first published

1974
President Richard M. Nixon resigns, succeeded by President Gerald R. Ford

1975
"A Chorus Line" by Marvin Hamlisch, lyrics by Edward Kleban

1976
Bicentennial of the United States

1976
Saul Bellow awarded the Nobel Prize in literature

There's no such thing as a free lunch

1976
Milton Friedman wins Nobel Prize in economics

1977
"Annie Hall" directed by Woody Allen wins Academy Award for Best Picture

1978
San Francisco Mayor George Moscone and Supervisor Harvey Milk assassinated

1978
Isaac Bashevis Singer awarded the Nobel Prize in literature

1979
President Jimmy Carter joins President Anwar el-Sadat of Egypt and Prime Minister Menachem Begin of Israel as they sign a Peace Treaty at the White House

שלום

Peace has come

ISRAELI PRIME MINISTER
MENACHEM BEGIN

1981
"On Women and Judaism" by Blu Greenberg

1982
Vietnam Veterans Memorial dedicated

1980
Ronald W. Reagan elected President

1983
Brighton Beach Memoirs" by Neil Simon, first of three biographical plays

1983
Central Conference of American Rabbis (Reform) adopts resolution on patrilineality, defining Jewish descent through either father or mother

...I lift my lamp beside the golden door!
EMMA LAZARUS

1983
"A Vanished World" photographed by Roman Vishniac

1983
"Yentl," film directed by Barbra Streisand, based on a short story by Isaac Bashevis Singer

1984
84 pianists play George Gershwin's "Rhapsody in Blue" at the Opening Ceremonies of the Games of the XXIII Olympiad Los Angeles

1985
"Sunday in the Park with George," Stephen Sondheim's musical, wins Pulitzer Prize for drama

1986
Centennial celebration of the Statue of Liberty

1986
Elie Wiesel awarded Nobel Peace Prize

6 5 4 3 2 1

1986
Dr. Judith Resnik, first Jewish astronaut, killed along with six colleagues in Challenger explosion

1987
"Black Monday"
Wall Street crash

CRASH!

1989
Composer Irving Berlin dies at age 101

40

**Illustration of British
band leader Geraldo
for the *White Elephant
Celebrity Cookbook.*
(Collins, 1973)**

CHARNOS FINESSE

sheer
seamless
micromesh

Illustration for Charnos
hosiery packaging.
Art Director: Tom Wolsey.

42

Illustrations for *Thousand Makers of the 20th Century, The Sunday Times Magazine.* Art Director: Michael Rand.

ABOVE: Benito Mussolini.
OPPOSITE: Ivan Pavlov.

TARAXACUM OFFICINALE

45

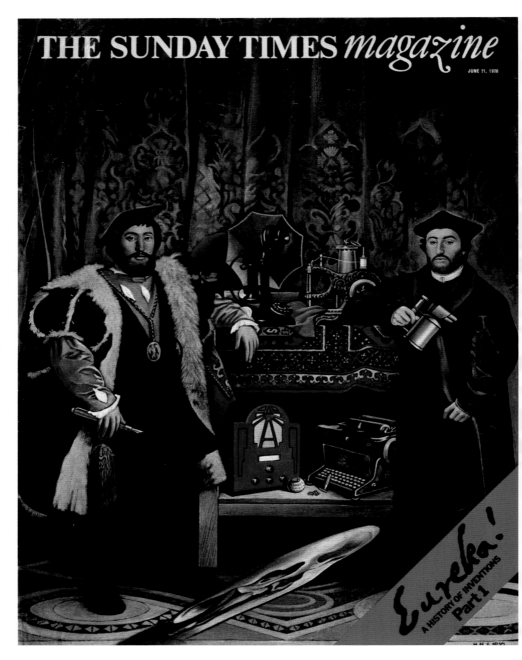

After working as an illustrator for *The Sunday Times* for some years, I was asked by the magazine's art director, Michael Rand, and the Special Projects Editor, Mark Boxer, to design *Eureka! A History of Inventions*, a supplement published in twelve weekly parts.

Cover for Part 1 of *Eureka!*
A History of Inventions, based
on the painting *The Ambassdors*
by Hans Holbein.
Illustration: Paul Davis.

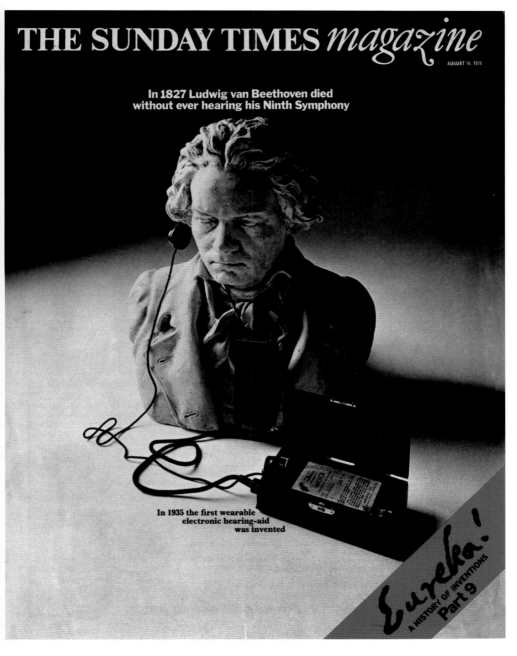

THE SUNDAY TIMES *magazine*

AUGUST 16, 1970

In 1827 Ludwig van Beethoven died
without ever hearing his Ninth Symphony

47

In 1935 the first wearable
electronic hearing-aid
was invented

Eureka!
A HISTORY OF INVENTIONS
Part 9

Cover for Part 9 of *Eureka!*
A History of Inventions,
The Sunday Times Magazine.

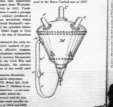

48

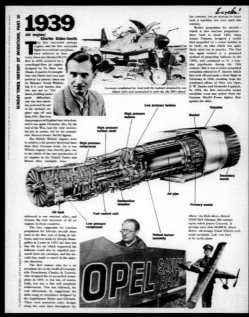

ABOVE: Pages from *Eureka!*
A History of Inventions.
Series Editor: Mark Boxer;
Designer: Arnold Schwartzman;
Design Assistant: Chris Bower.

OPPOSITE: Cover of Part 6 of
Eureka! A History of Inventions,
The Sunday Times Magazine.

49

I had commissioned illustrations of inventors Logie Baird (television) and Marconi (radio) for the cover of Part 6. Due to a last-minute change in the magazine's pagination, these inventions were re-scheduled to appear in two separate future issues. With only hours to go before the deadline, I rapidly drew this portrait of Thomas Edison and placed what was the beginnings of my gramophone needle tin collection in the background, which I happened to have with me at the magazine.

I had organized a number of locations and set-ups for the shoot to promote the Rolling Stones' new album, *Sticky Fingers*.

Unfortunately the group arrived so late in the day, that I had to quickly come up with a new idea. I suggested that Mick strip off and hold the sleeve – jeans with a practical zip – in a strategic position. As I was given only one prototype of Andy Warhol's sleeve design, each member of the band was photographed separately.

The finished image was such a success that it was copied by other groups, and the greatly sought-after, life-size cut-out of Mick Jagger could be seen prominently displayed in the windows of stores and residences alike.

Promotion campaign
for The Rolling Stones'
Sticky Fingers album.
Sleeve design: Andy Warhol.
Photograph: David Montgomery.

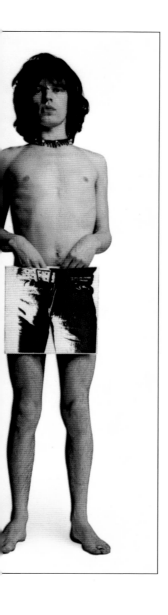

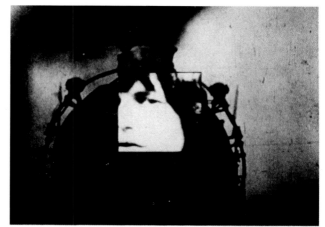

51

ABOVE: Stills from the cinema trailer promoting The Rolling Stones' album *All Down The Line*, incorporating imagery created by Robert Frank.

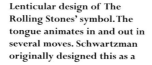

Lenticular design of The Rolling Stones' symbol. The tongue animates in and out in several moves. Schwartzman originally designed this as a record label but it proved to be impractical to affix to the discs, and was later produced as a button.

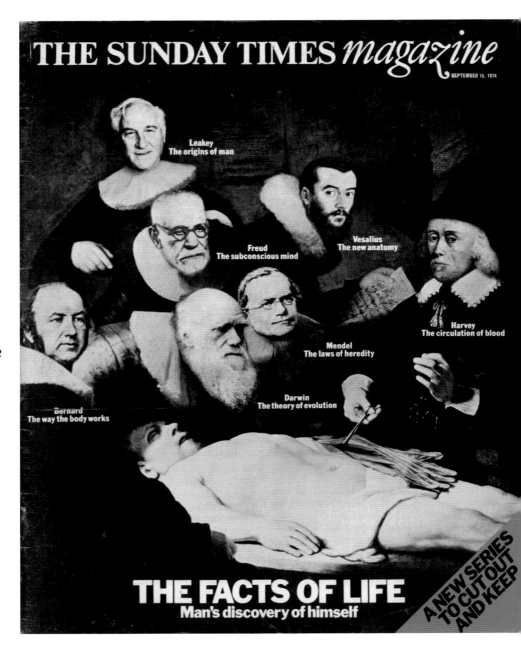

THE SUNDAY TIMES *magazine*

SEPTEMBER 15, 1974

Leakey
The origins of man

Freud
The subconscious mind

Vesalius
The new anatomy

Harvey
The circulation of blood

Mendel
The laws of heredity

Bernard
The way the body works

Darwin
The theory of evolution

A NEW SERIES
TO CUT OUT
AND KEEP

THE FACTS OF LIFE
Man's discovery of himself

Cover for the first issue of
The Sunday Times Magazine's
special weekly supplement,
*The Facts of Life: Man's Discovery
of Himself*, 1974. The participants
in Rembrandt's painting

The Anatomy Class have been
transposed to those of the great
luminaries of medical science.
Editor: Peter Ryan;
Associate Editors:
Mark Boxer, Robert Lacey;

Art Director/Designer:
Arnold Schwartzman;
Assistant Art Directors:
Sarah Bee and Celia Stothard.
D&AD Silver Award for Most
Outstanding Special Series, 1975.

ABOVE: Pages from *The Facts of Life: Man's Discovery of Himself.* Illustrator: Seymour Chwast.
BELOW: The hard cover binder, decorated with Eadweard Muybridge's *Man in Motion.*

After leaving television for advertising, I continued to work with some of the groups I had met on RSG!. One of these, The Who, composed and recorded a track for me for a series of cinema commercials for Coca-Cola, for the grand total of £400.

Around that time, a friend, David Puttnam, a photographers' agent (now Lord Puttnam), came to me with a proposal from the Beatles who wished to write a song about Coca-Cola due to the beverage's appeal to a young audience. By the time the request reached the company's headquarters in Atlanta, the Beatles had gone off to visit the Maharishi in India.

One Coke commercial involved a shoot in St. James's Park, filming geese taking flight in the cold early morning mist. After several successful takes our crew moved on to shoot Big Ben as its hands reached eight o'clock. While waiting for the appointed hour, the client accidentally tripped over the tripod, crashing the camera to the ground, its magazine breaking open, and reeling out the film containing our precious previous scenes across Westminster Bridge!

Television commercial for Coca-Cola. A bottle made of frozen "Coke" melts to fill a glass, filmed in time lapse.

It took Schwartzman six hours to film, exposing a frame every three seconds.

Vroeger, als de mensen griep hadden, namen ze AntiGrippine met een hete grok.

Net als tegenwoordig, want AntiGrippine stilt de pijn, weert de koorts, bevat

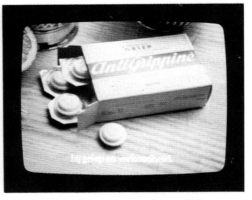

vitamine C en is bovendien opwekkend. AntiGrippine werkt probaat. Al járen.

Frames from a Dutch anti-flu pharmaceutical television commercial for National Publiciteits Onderneming BV.

Concept, production design and direction by Schwartzman.

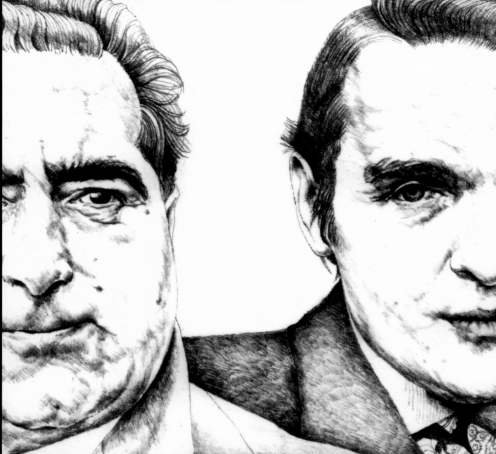

Since my student days, it had been my dream to illustrate for the *Radio Times* magazine because of its high standard of illustrations. This ambition was fulfilled when later I became a regular contributor.

As the Art Director wished me to portray both stars in the very small space allotted, I decided to draw just half a face of each of the two well-known actors, thus reflecting the play's title, *The One-Eyed Monster*.

Illustration for the *Radio Times* for the BBC drama programme, *The One-Eyed Monster*. Art Director: David Driver.

ELEPHANTA:

The Magazine of The White Elephant Club

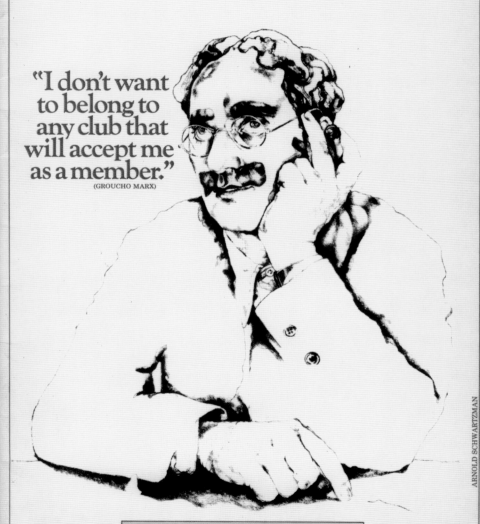

"I don't want
to belong to
any club that
will accept me
as a member."
(GROUCHO MARX)

ARNOLD SCHWARTZMAN

AN ALBUM OF PEOPLE AND PLACES

THE DESIGNERS FILM UNIT. 1 OLD COMPTON
STREET. LONDON. W1V 5PH. Tel: 01-437 9450
Consultants: JIM BAKER, ARNOLD SCHWARTZMAN,
Bookbinder Silverstein and Baker Ltd. Registered
Office: 27 Blandford Street. London. W1H 3AD.
Directors: J.C. Baker, C.P.L. Bullmore. Registered
in England No 989533 VAT Registration 232 1800 11

**Business card for The Designers
Film Unit, in the style of a
cigarette card. The front of the
card also served as the company's
letterhead by being slotted into
each sheet.**

Pʜɪʟɪᴘs was formed in Britain in January 1925, although the parent company originated in Eindhoven in 1891 to manufacture filament lamps.
The type 2007 high impedance electro-magnetic speaker was one of the first Philips introduced in this country in 1926. It was initially used with the 2514 receiver, itself one of the first mains sets sold in quantity on the British market.

Model: Claudia Dantonny. Clothes J.M. Rowe: Mood Prince, Hat Bremmen.

Pʜɪʟɪᴘs introduced the first rotary action mains shaver in the United Kingdom in October 1949. Type No. SC7739.

*Model: * Chrissie Keating, Cancel Erbiston, Kim. Clothes Belts & Hats; Music d'Europe Illustration Jean Lagarrigue.*

W T F S S M T W T F S S M T W T F S S M T W T F S S M T W T
1 2 3 4 5 6 7 8 9 10 11 12 13 14 15 16 17 18 19 20 21 22 23 24 25 26 27 28 29 30 31
January 1975

M T W T F S S M T W T F S S M T W T F S S M T W T F S S M T
1 2 3 4 5 6 7 8 9 10 11 12 13 14 15 16 17 18 19 20 21 22 23 24 25 26 27 28 29 30
September 1975

Pʜɪʟɪᴘs production of domestic radio receivers and television sets was halted shortly after the start of WW II. by 1944 the scarcity of radio receivers was such that a basic design for a Wartime Civilian Receiver was drawn up using the minimum materials and labour. Philips, along with most other British radio firms, produced this set which was identified only by a code number (Philips was U8).

Model: Aurore Clement, Berris Sylvie, Paul North. Clothes Les Mures d'Europe, Coiffeur de Temps et des 30-25; Hair: Estela, Jewellery La Foire Rouge, Location Pan Pan.

Pʜɪʟɪᴘs introduced a projection television receiver in 1937. As early as 1927 the parent company in Eindhoven built and tested a crystal controlled short wave transmitter operating on 30.92 metres, using their own water cooled valves. Reception extended as far as the East Indies, some 10,000 miles away. Later that year Philips co-operated in relaying the first BBC Empire Broadcast.

Model: Carole Singleton, Paul North. Airball La Forte Rous.

T W T F S S M T W T F S S M T W T F S S M T W T F S S M T W T
1 2 3 4 5 6 7 8 9 10 11 12 13 14 15 16 17 18 19 20 21 22 23 24 25 26 27 28 29 30 31
July 1975

T F S S M T W T F S S M T W T F S S M T W T F S S M T W T F S
1 2 3 4 5 6 7 8 9 10 11 12 13 14 15 16 17 18 19 20 21 22 23 24 25 26 27 28 29 30 31
May 1975

Philips Electrical's Golden Jubilee

Cover design for *Quiet As A Nun,*
by Antonia Fraser.
(Penguin Books, 1978.)
Photograph: Anthony Blake.

LEN DEIGHTON & ARNOLD SCHWARTZMAN
AIRSHIPWRECK

61

... getting that wonderful book, I learned a lot. Best regards, Henry.

— HENRY WOLF, 1992

ABOVE: Cover of *Airshipwreck*, co-authored with Len Deighton. Photograph: Harry Peccinotti. (Jonathan Cape, 1978).

BELOW: The record insert featured a recording of the radio broadcast of the Hindenburg disaster in 1936.

Seasons greetings from Arnold Schwartzman 7260 Hillside Ave., Hollywood, CA 90046

62

One of my first assignments on joining Saul Bass & Associates in Los Angeles was to design a poster announcing the new Girl Scouts symbol. I decided to interpret the symbol photographically, and contacted a local troupe, requesting a few girl scouts to volunteer as models.

We drove up into Griffith Park in the Hollywood Hills, where I waited for the magic "golden hour" before taking the photograph. Meanwhile, I was approached by a suspicious Park Ranger, concerned about my motives for being there with these young girls!

The Hollywood sign serves as a
Christmas greetings card, 1978.

GIRL SCOUTS

Genocide

Following my departure from Saul Bass's company, on his recommendation the newly formed Simon Wiesenthal Center commissioned me to produce an audio-visual documentary on the subject of the Holocaust for its new museum.

As I progressed with this project, and discovered its magnitude, it grew in scope. I asked the noted historian Martin Gilbert to write the script, Elizabeth Taylor and Orson Welles to provide the narration, and composer Elmer Bernstein to write the music score. After receiving critical acclaim at its initial screenings, we decided to transfer the 21-projector production optically to a 35 mm Panavision film.

On completion, the film was submitted to the Academy for consideration, and subsequently *Genocide* was awarded the Oscar for Best Documentary Feature in 1982.

Dear Arnold, it was an amazing experience working with you. Much love, Elizabeth.

— ELIZABETH TAYLOR, 1982.

Congratulations. Even in Seville we knew you had won. Thanks for the kind words, Elmer.

—TELEGRAM FROM ELMER BERNSTEIN, 1982.

Schwartzman accepting his Best Documentary Feature

Genocide logotype rendered by Alan Peckolick.

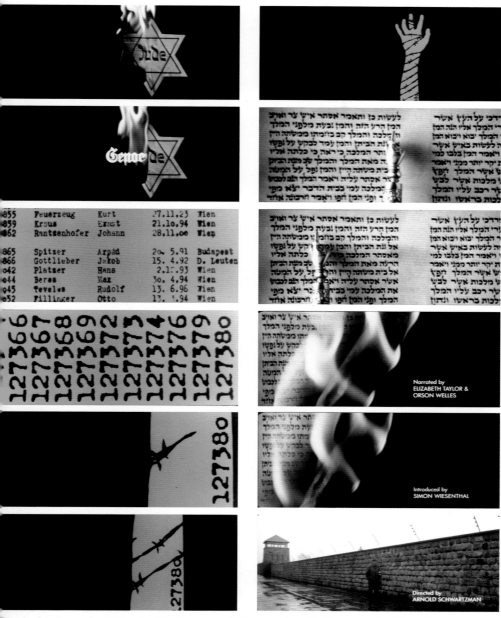

65

Genocide's _main title design is one of the most artistic seen in films for years, highly reminiscent of the magnificent titles once created by Saul Bass._

Frames from the opening
title sequence for _Genocide._
Simon Wiesenthal Center,
Los Angeles.

*Your contributions to the Games of the XXIII Olympiad were excellent, and
provided much of the direction that led to their success.*

– PETER V. UEBERROTH, PRESIDENT, LOS ANGELES OLYMPIC ORGANIZING COMMITTEE, 1985.

66

During my tenure as Design Director for
the 1984 Olympic Games in Los Angeles,
I commissioned a series of commemorative
posters, each depicting an Olympic event. As
none of the distinguished designers chose to
interpret track cycling, I decided to design
the poster myself.

At that time I was adapting the Olympic
symbol on a daily basis, and was so locked
into this motif that the wheels idea came
to mind almost instantly.

I located three Olympic hopefuls and
arranged to photograph them at the newly

completed Velodrome. I showed them a sketch
of the result I wished to achieve before they
started to circle the track in formation. There
was only one part of the track where its
high wall provided a suitable background,
restricting me to photographing the cyclists
only once per circuit.

After about fifty laps, I asked the athletes
if they were prepared to continue. They
readily agreed, not knowing that they would
have to complete more than three hundred
laps before I felt confident that I had got
the shot!

Schwartzman presents his design
for the Olympic Arts Festival logo
to Peter V. Ueberroth, President,
Los Angeles Olympic
Organizing Committee.

SIGNATURE SERIES

Arnold Schwartzman

Designed & Photographed by Arnold Schwartzman

© 1980 L.A. Olympic Organizing Committee   TM

Cycling poster, one of the
"Signature Series" official
posters for the 1984 Olympic
Games, Los Angeles.

© 1983 L.A. Olympic Committee

68

ABOVE: The Olympic Spirit Team symbol utilises the 1984 Olympic pictograms spelling out the Roman numerals XXIII denoting the Games of the 23rd Olympiad.

BELOW: Olympic Arts Festival symbol. Robert Miles Runyon's 1984 Olympic Games symbol forms the "A" of Arts, rendered in Sussman/Prejza's "Festive Federalism" colour palette.

RIGHT: Olympic rings form the numerals 88 for the International Olympic Committee's 88th Session logo. 1984.

FAR RIGHT: Coloured ribbons form the numerals 88 in Schwartzman's original sketch (actual size) for the IOC's 88th Session poster. Rhythmic gymnastics was recognised as an official event in 1984.

69

ABOVE: Official invitation to the Games of the XXIIIrd Olympiad. The Olympic motto provides the initials "USA", which are highlighted in a clear varnish on the vellum overlay.

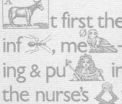

Sequences poster for the
Simpson Paper Company, 1986.
Art Director: James Cross.

Design Arnold Schwartzman · Lithography Anderson Printing · Paper Simpson Sundance Felt, Curl Grey Cover 65lb · Design Consultants Cross Associates · Printed in U.S.A.

r, full
oaths,
ke the
onour,
a quar-
ubble
in the

THE
SA

"As
you
like
it."

As you like it.

**AND THEN THE
JUSTICE, IN
FAIR ROUND
BELLY WITH GOOD
CAPON LIN'D, WITH
EYES SEVERE AND
BEARD OF FORMAL
CUT, FULL OF WISE
SAWS AND MODERN
INSTANCES: AND SO
HE PLAYS HIS PART.**

AND WOMEN
; THEY HAVE
HEIR ENTRAN
ME PLAYS MANY PARTS,
SEVEN AGES :

The sixth age shifts into the lean and slipper'd pantaloon, with spectacles on nose and pouch on side, his youthful hose, well sav'd, a world too wide for his shrunk shank; and his big manly voice, turning again toward childish treble, pipes and whistles in his sound.

Last scene of all, that ends this strange eventful history, is second childishness & mere oblivion; sans teeth, sans eyes, sans taste, sans everything.

ces

A typographic triumph.

Steven (Spielberg) and I think your film is a masterpiece.
– ROBERTO BENIGNI'S COMMENT ON *GENOCIDE*, LONDON, 1999.

72

1990
Berlin Wall
dismantled

1990
A call by followers of the
Lubavicher Rebbe, Menachem Schneerson

WE WANT
MOSHIACH NOW!

Gay and Jewish, and proud of both.

1990
Meir Kahane,
founder of the
Jewish Defense
League,
assassinated

Never again!

1990
Composer
Leonard Bernstein
dies

YES I CAN
THE STORY OF SAMMY DAVIS, JR.

1990
Entertainer
Sammy Davis Jr.
dies

1991
War in Persian Gulf
President George Bush
orders "Operation
Desert Storm"

NY RIOTS

LA RIOTS

Can we all get along?
RODNEY KING

1991
Clash between
Hasidic Jews and
black community
in Brooklyn

1992
Los Angeles riots after
acquittal of four white
police officers charged
with beating black
motorist Rodney King

1994
"Schindler's List,"
directed by
Steven Spielberg
wins Academy
Award for
Best Picture

6.6

1994
Los Angeles
earthquake

1993
Prime Minister
Yitzhak Rabin
and P.L.O.
Chairman
Yasser Arafat
sign peace
accord

1997
J. Paul Getty
Museum opens
in Los Angeles,
designed by
architect
Richard Meier

1997
Madeline Albright,
first female
U.S. Secretary
of State,
discloses her
Jewish ancestry

1993
Terrorist bomb
attack under
World Trade
Center twin
towers in New
York City

1995
Terrorists bomb
Oklahoma City
Federal building

1995
Israeli
Prime Minister
Yitzhak Rabin
assassinated

1993
FBI siege
of Branch
Davidian
cult head-
quarters

WACO

*Whoever
saves
one life,
saves
the world
entire.*
THE TALMUD

1998
DreamWorks
releases
"The Prince
of Egypt," an
animated film
based on the
story of Moses

1993
United States
Holocaust
Memorial
Museum opens
in Washington

*Ye shall hallow the fiftieth year ...
it shall be a jubilee unto you.*
EXODUS 25:10

1998
The State of Israel
celebrates its 50th
anniversary

1996
Skirball Cultural Center opens,
designed by Moshe Safdie

As we stand at the edge of the 21st century, let us begin anew with energy and hope...
PRESIDENT BILL CLINTON, INAUGURAL ADDRESS

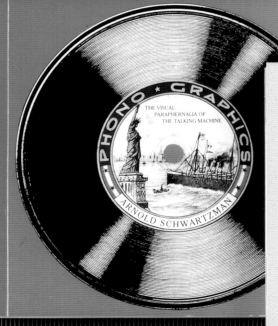

DESIGNAGE

The Art of the Decorative Sign

ARNOLD SCHWARTZMAN

Your "Designage" is absolutely beautiful and amazing. You will single-handedly bring back traditional and decorative typography. Congratulations. — SEYMOUR CHWAST

It will be the definitive book on the subject for some time.
— GEORGE TSCHERNY

What a splendid and useful book. — MILTON GLASER

Thank you for your lovely book. One could learn a lot about design from the dead... Best, Paul

— LETTER FROM PAUL RAND REGARDING *GRAVEN IMAGES*, 1993.

Schwartzman's photograph of a prayer hall at the Jewish cemetery in Ferrara, Italy, from *Graven Images: Graphic Motifs of the Jewish Gravestone.*

These photos of Jewish gravestones offer achingly beautiful images that evoke a flood of questions, association, sadness, and a simple awe that lingers.
— SAUL BASS'S REVIEW OF *GRAVEN IMAGES*, *GRAPHIS*, JULY/AUGUST 1993.

Jewish cemetery, Bobowa, Poland

Man then goes out
to his work, to his
labor until the
evening.
PSALMS 104:23

In 1808, Napoleon
imposed a law
requiring Jews
to adopt a family
name, in
contradiction to
their traditional
practice of using
only first names.
Many took the
name of their
hometown or that
of their profession.

Right and
pages 120 and 121
Tools of a trade,
such as a pair of
scales for a money-
changer and a plow
for a farmer, a ship
(representing the
Schiff family), and
biblical motifs are
all to be found in
this medieval
cemetery dating
from 12th
Battonstrasse
Cemetery,
Frankfurt am Main

ABOVE: Spreads from
Graven Images:
Graphic Motifs of the
Jewish Gravestone.
(Horn, N. Abrams 1993)

OPPOSITE: The Western Wall,
Jerusalem, one of several of
Schwartzman's photographs
published in *The Synagogue.*
(Rhaidon, 1995)

TABLE OF CONTENTS

INTRODUCTION 8

PHONOGRAPHS
AND CYLINDER
BOXES 16

DISC PLAYERS 22

AMPLIFYING
HORNS 28

POSTCARDS 46

ADVERTISING 48

RECORD
LABELS AND
SLEEVES 68

PHONOGRAPH
NEEDLE TINS 72

PICTURE RECORDS 110

32

Opposite:
Collection of needle
tins displaying
horned disc players.
COLLECTION OF
THE AUTHOR

This page:
Victor IV
phonograph
with nickel horn,
1902–1920.
COLLECTION OF
JOE URBANOWICH

33

PICTURE RECORDS

The introduction of flexible vinyl records brought with it a new
medium for the commercial artist.

Art Deco style
illustrations cover
the complete surface
of these French
Ultraphone picture
records, 1930's.
COLLECTION OF
MARTIN AND JILLIANA
RAINWURMBRECH

110

111

**Spreads from *Phono-Graphics:
The Visual Paraphernalia
of the Talking Machine.*
Photographs: Garry Brod.
(Chronicle Books, 1993)**

As a member of the United States Motion Picture Centennial Committee, I was asked to submit a stamp design to the U.S. Postal Service for consideration. I saw the similarity between Thomas Edison's grid of frames of his first motion picture image, *Fred Ott's Sneeze,* and a sheet of postage stamps. The response from the Postmaster General's office was that they no longer commemorate 100th anniversaries!

Among the pile of new commemorative WWII picture books, this one may do the best job of hitting all the emotional notes at once. With a filmmaker's eye, Schwartzman, an Englishman, beautifully mixes the evocative knick-knacks of the Home Front... This inspired scrapbook accompanies a new film by Mr. Schwartzman.

– *AMERICAN HERITAGE*, REVIEW OF *LIBERATION*, DECEMBER 1994.

ABOVE: Endpapers for the book
Liberation .
(Museum of Tolerance, 1994)

The visual philosophy that I gained as a child looking at the picture comparisons in *Lilliput* magazines inspired the above endpaper images.

ottobre
october
octobre
oktober
octubre

1997

84

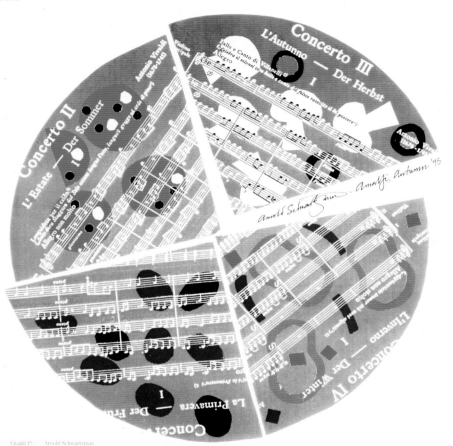

Vivaldi Pizza / Arnold Schwartzman

Members of the Alliance Graphique Internationale are usually asked to contribute a design themed to the annual Congress's location. In Amalfi, Italy, the subject was pizza. My concept was a metaphor for *Quatro*

Staggione **(Four Seasons) pizza, adapting the music score from Vivaldi's *Four Seasons*. Later, the design was chosen for a calendar.**

Art Directors: Heinz Weibl with Armando Milani for PuntoGrafico, Italy.

Monday	Tuesday	Wednesday	Thursday	Friday	Saturday	Sunday

JANUARY 1998

WOOD & WOOD MAKE SIGNS

85

Monday	Tuesday	Wednesday	Thursday	Friday	Saturday	Sunday

DECEMBER 1998

WOOD & WOOD MAKE SIGNS

Calendar for Wood & Wood
sign makers, 1998.
Art Director: Alan Fletcher.

365 different door numbers
photographed around the world
by Schwartzman make up the

Spreads from *Designage:
The Art of the Decorative Sign*
(Chronicle Books, 1998)

**This delightful work is the finest in Chronicle Books'
series of little 8"x10" art reference books**

+
10

8 8

7 7

-10 -10

2 0 0 3

A game of deck shuffleboard
becomes a Christmas tree for
a proposed greetings card for a
cruiseship's concessionaire.

ARNOLD SCHWARTZMAN 9 BONHAM HOUSE...

107 LADBROKE ROAD LONDON W11   01·727·1994

S c h • w • a

Schh... you-know-who.
— SCHWEPPES ADVERTISEMENT

It's cleve

'Do you spell it with a "V" or a "W"?'
inquired the judge.
— CHARLES DICKENS

Business and personal logotypes,
from the 60s onwards.

ARNOLD SCHWARTZMAN
— PRODUCTIONS —

89

t·z·man

art?
ARD KIPLING

*When a man is tired of London
he is tired of life.*
— DR. SAMUEL JOHNSON

*Thou whoreson zed!
Thou unnecessary letter!*
— WILLIAM SHAKESPEARE

...I love your letterhead!
— LOU DORFSMAN, 1979.

ABOVE: Tequila bottle label, based on traditional Mexican paper cuts.
BELOW: Wine label, *To Be Or Not To Be,* for a fundraising project for London's Shakespeare Globe Theatre. Shakespeare's well-known line can be read continuously on the wraparound labels, however displayed, 1997.

OPPOSITE: Poster for a symposium on the works of William Shakespeare.

Shakespeare,
Passion
and the Body Politic

Neapolitan Gestures No.3
"BEAUTY"

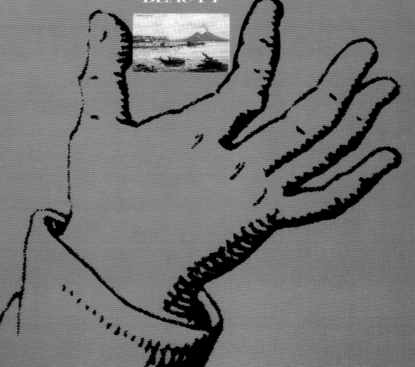

Poster for *Napoli 99.*

U C L A EXTENSION WINTER QUARTER BEGINS JANUARY 9, 1999

www.unex.ucla.edu

U C L A

EXTENSION

Winter
Quarter
begins
January 9,
1999

I named my talk on Saul Bass to the American
Institute of Graphic Arts, Texas, *Anatomy of
a Mentor*, a play on words on *Anatomy of a
Murder*, and adapted Saul's iconic image that
he had created for the film to frame his name.

Cover design for UCLA Extension
Course, 1999, a visual metaphor
for the word "Extension".
Art Director: Inju Sturgeon, UCLA.

OPPOSITE: Poster for a talk on
the work of Saul Bass, 1998.
American Institute of Graphic
Arts, Austin, Texas.

The American Institute of Graphic Arts | Austin presents

ANATOMY
OF A MENTOR

NOLD SCHWARTZMAN on SAUL BASS

red film titles include:

T SIDE STORY
E FEAR
MAN WITH THE GOLDEN ARM
CHO
TH BY NORTHWEST
TIGO
OF THE ROSES
DFELLAS
K ON THE WILD SIDE

nesday 9 December 1998
7:30 pm reception
9 pm lecture

Dobie Theatre
& Guadalupe Street

sented with the Austin Film Society

SAUL
BASS

"Saul once told me that he would have
liked to have been an archeologist...
but in reality what Saul really wanted
to be was Saul Bass—and so did I!"

Anatomy of a Mentor, by Arnold Schwartzman
baseline International Typographics Journal
Issue 22, 1996

As a Governor and past Chairman of the British Academy of Film and Television Arts/ Los Angeles®, I have designed a number of pieces for the Academy, such as the invitations and programme covers for the Academy's Britannia Award® banquets.

The year we honoured James Bond films producer Albert "Cubby" Broccoli, I created a visual metaphor for the celebrated producer by placing a stalk of broccoli on a plate decorated with the "007" logo.

For the 1998 John Travolta event, I utilised John's "signature" dance gesture, last seen in the film *Pulp Fiction*, to form the letter V of Travolta.

Dear Arnold, Thank you for putting together the wonderful tribute journal for my Britannia Award honor. It is a suiting keepsake for me to always remember a wonderful evening by. Warmly, John.
— JOHN TRAVOLTA, 1998.

96

ABOVE: Britannia Award Banquet invitation and menu, honouring James Bond producer Albert "Cubby" Broccoli, 1989.

OPPOSITE: Cover of Britannia Award Banquet journal, honouring John Travolta, 1998.

The Los Angeles Chapter of the
American Institute of Graphic Arts
(AIGA) in collaboration with the
Royal Society of Arts (RSA),
the British Consulate-General
Los Angeles and the British American
Chamber of Commerce Los Angeles
invites you to spend an evening
pondering the "Stuff & Nonsense"
of contemporary graphic design
on both sides of the pond.

In a rare appearance in the United
States, design legend and Pentagram
founder, Royal Designer for Industry
Alan Fletcher RDI.

The best of British continues
with presentations by two British
Los Angeles-based designers,
Clive Piercy and
Michael Worthington.

*Fletcher means 'maker of arrows'
... a designer whose ability to hit
the target again and again with
such clarity and purpose has now
become legendary.*
BEWARE WET PAINT

10·21·99

cing a talk by
for the Royal
and the

& NonSense

rsday, October 21, 1999
eption, 6:30-7:30 P.M.
gram, 7:30 P.M.

en Theater
Pacific Design Theater
7 Melrose Avenue
t Hollywood, CA 90069

VP: Reserve early.
event will sell out!
nent (check or credit card)
be received by October 15.

Ticket Information:
Members $15
Non-Members $25
Member Students $10
Non-Member Students $15

Send check to:
American Institute of Graphic Arts
Los Angeles Chapter
116 The Plaza Pasadena
Pasadena, CA 91101

Or call 818.952.2442 for
credit card transactions.

E-mail or fax number required
for confirmation notification.

For information regarding
AIGA membership or programs,
call 818.952.2442
or visit www.aiga-la.com

As a Fellow of Britain's Royal Society of Arts, I was asked to assist in coordinating several lectures in Los Angeles for visiting Royal Designers for Industry (RDI).

One of the speakers was my good friend Alan Fletcher. The meaning of his name, "maker of arrows", inspired my design for the poster announcing his talk.

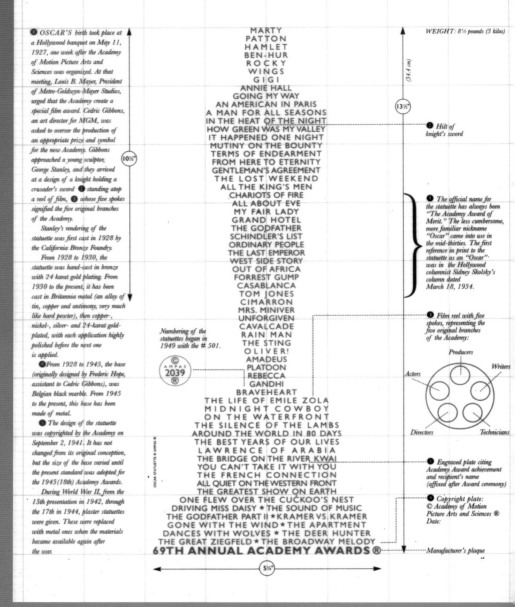

1 OSCAR'S *birth took place at a Hollywood banquet on May 11, 1927, one week after the Academy of Motion Picture Arts and Sciences was organized. At that meeting, Louis B. Mayer, President of Metro-Goldwyn-Mayer Studios, urged that the Academy create a special film award. Cedric Gibbons, an art director for MGM, was asked to oversee the production of an appropriate prize and symbol for the new Academy. Gibbons approached a young sculptor, George Stanley, and they arrived at a design of a knight holding a crusader's sword* **2** *standing atop a reel of film,* **3** *whose five spokes signified the five original branches of the Academy.*

Stanley's rendering of the statuette was first cast in 1928 by the California Bronze Foundry.

From 1928 to 1930, the statuette was hand-cast in bronze with 24 karat gold plating. From 1930 to the present, it has been cast in Britannia metal (an alloy of tin, copper and antimony, very much like hard pewter), then copper-, nickel-, silver- and 24-karat gold-plated, with each application highly polished before the next one is applied.

4 *From 1928 to 1945, the base (originally designed by Frederic Hope, assistant to Cedric Gibbons), was Belgian black marble. From 1945 to the present, this base has been made of metal.*

5 *The design of the statuette was copyrighted by the Academy on September 2, 1941. It has not changed from its original conception, but the size of the base varied until the present standard was adopted for the 1945 (18th) Academy Awards.*

During World War II, from the 15th presentation in 1942, through the 17th in 1944, plaster statuettes were given. These were replaced with metal ones when the materials became available again after the war.

WEIGHT: 8½ pounds (3 kilos)

(34.4 cm)

13½"

2 *Hilt of knight's sword*

10½"

1 *The official name for the statuette has always been "The Academy Award of Merit." The less cumbersome, more familiar nickname "Oscar" came into use in the mid-thirties. The first reference in print to the statuette as an "Oscar" was in the Hollywood columnist Sidney Skolsky's column dated March 18, 1934.*

3 *Film reel with five spokes, representing the five original branches of the Academy:*

Producers
Writers
Actors
Directors
Technicians

Numbering of the statuettes began in 1949 with the # 501.

© AMPAS 2039 ®

OSCAR STATUETTE © AMPAS ®

MARTY
PATTON
HAMLET
BEN-HUR
ROCKY
WINGS
GIGI
ANNIE HALL
GOING MY WAY
AN AMERICAN IN PARIS
A MAN FOR ALL SEASONS
IN THE HEAT OF THE NIGHT
HOW GREEN WAS MY VALLEY
IT HAPPENED ONE NIGHT
MUTINY ON THE BOUNTY
TERMS OF ENDEARMENT
FROM HERE TO ETERNITY
GENTLEMAN'S AGREEMENT
THE LOST WEEKEND
ALL THE KING'S MEN
CHARIOTS OF FIRE
ALL ABOUT EVE
MY FAIR LADY
GRAND HOTEL
THE GODFATHER
SCHINDLER'S LIST
ORDINARY PEOPLE
THE LAST EMPEROR
WEST SIDE STORY
OUT OF AFRICA
FORREST GUMP
CASABLANCA
TOM JONES
CIMARRON
MRS. MINIVER
UNFORGIVEN
CAVALCADE
RAIN MAN
THE STING
OLIVER!
AMADEUS
PLATOON
REBECCA
GANDHI
BRAVEHEART
THE LIFE OF EMILE ZOLA
MIDNIGHT COWBOY
ON THE WATERFRONT
THE SILENCE OF THE LAMBS
AROUND THE WORLD IN 80 DAYS
THE BEST YEARS OF OUR LIVES
LAWRENCE OF ARABIA
THE BRIDGE ON THE RIVER KWAI
YOU CAN'T TAKE IT WITH YOU
THE FRENCH CONNECTION
ALL QUIET ON THE WESTERN FRONT
THE GREATEST SHOW ON EARTH
ONE FLEW OVER THE CUCKOO'S NEST
DRIVING MISS DAISY ★ THE SOUND OF MUSIC
THE GODFATHER PART II ★ KRAMER VS. KRAMER
GONE WITH THE WIND ★ THE APARTMENT
DANCES WITH WOLVES ★ THE DEER HUNTER
THE GREAT ZIEGFELD ★ THE BROADWAY MELODY
69TH ANNUAL ACADEMY AWARDS ®

5 *Engraved plate citing Academy Award achievement and recipient's name (affixed after Award ceremony)*

4 *Copyright plate:*
© Academy of Motion Picture Arts and Sciences ®
Date:

Manufacturer's plaque

5¼"

When Saul Bass, who had designed five of the Academy Awards' commemorative posters, died in 1996, the Academy asked me if I would "take up the reins".

The Academy's President and Executive Director were unanimous in their acceptance of my design depicting the previous 68 Best Film titles in the shape of an Oscar statuette. On seeing this design, the Executive Director exclaimed: "Thank heavens for *Gigi*, otherwise Oscar wouldn't have a neck!"

ABOVE: Historic facts and figures pertaining to the Oscar statuette are printed on the vellum fly-leaf of the 1997 programme.

OPPOSITE: Commemorative poster for the 69th Annual Academy Awards, 1997. Academy of Motion Picture Arts and Sciences.

OSCAR

MARTY
PATTON
HAMLET
BEN-HUR
ROCKY
WINGS
GIGI
ANNIE HALL
GOING MY WAY
AN AMERICAN IN PARIS
A MAN FOR ALL SEASONS
IN THE HEAT OF THE NIGHT
HOW GREEN WAS MY VALLEY
IT HAPPENED ONE NIGHT
MUTINY ON THE BOUNTY
TERMS OF ENDEARMENT
FROM HERE TO ETERNITY
GENTLEMAN'S AGREEMENT
THE LOST WEEKEND
ALL THE KING'S MEN
CHARIOTS OF FIRE
ALL ABOUT EVE
MY FAIR LADY
GRAND HOTEL
THE GODFATHER
SCHINDLER'S LIST
ORDINARY PEOPLE
THE LAST EMPEROR
WEST SIDE STORY
OUT OF AFRICA
FORREST GUMP
CASABLANCA
TOM JONES
CIMARRON
MRS. MINIVER
UNFORGIVEN
CAVALCADE
RAIN MAN
THE STING
OLIVER!
AMADEUS
PLATOON
REBECCA
GANDHI
BRAVEHEART
THE LIFE OF EMILE ZOLA
MIDNIGHT COWBOY
ON THE WATERFRONT
THE SILENCE OF THE LAMBS
AROUND THE WORLD IN 80 DAYS
THE BEST YEARS OF OUR LIVES
LAWRENCE OF ARABIA
THE BRIDGE ON THE RIVER KWAI
YOU CAN'T TAKE IT WITH YOU
THE FRENCH CONNECTION
ALL QUIET ON THE WESTERN FRONT
THE GREATEST SHOW ON EARTH
ONE FLEW OVER THE CUCKOO'S NEST
DRIVING MISS DAISY ★ THE SOUND OF MUSIC
THE GODFATHER PART II ★ KRAMER VS. KRAMER
GONE WITH THE WIND ★ THE APARTMENT
DANCES WITH WOLVES ★ THE DEER HUNTER
THE GREAT ZIEGFELD ★ THE BROADWAY MELODY
69TH ANNUAL ACADEMY AWARDS®

102

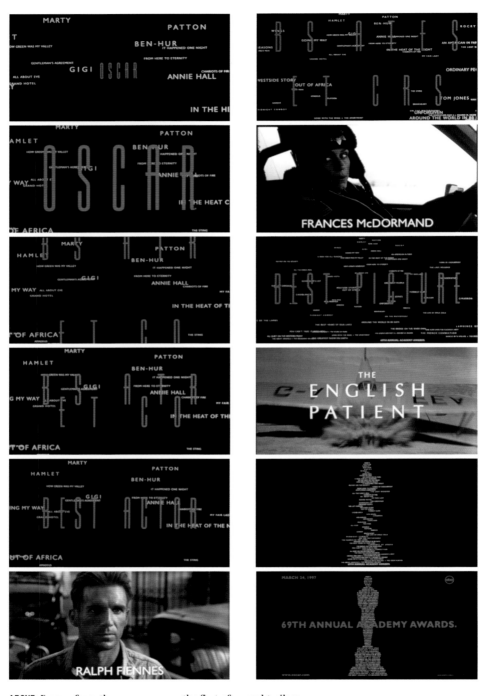

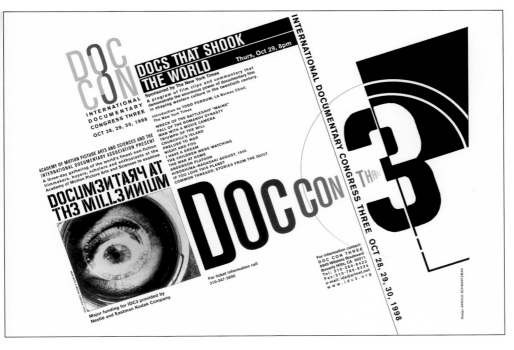

For the Third Annual Documentary Congress, I condensed the event's title to "DocCon", and re-named the International Documentary Association's annual October conference "Doctober". The event was later moved to September!

ABOVE: Half page advertisement in *The New York Times* for the 3rd International Documentary Congress.

BELOW: Logos for the 3rd and 4th (postponed) International Documentary Congresses.

ABOVE: Technicians prepare the neon sign for the red carpet entrance to the 70th Academy Awards presentation, Los Angeles, 1998.
Photograph: Long Photography.

OPPOSITE: Commemorative poster for the 70th Annual Academy Awards.

OSCAR

70TH ANNUAL ACADEMY AWARDS

ABOVE: Vellum "belly band" slips over a foil-stamped menu cover for the Academy Awards Governors Ball, 1999.

BELOW: Menu cover and spreads for the Academy's Governors Ball pays tribute to the cigarette card albums of the 1930s. Spreads show tipped-in photographs of Academy honourees.

OPPOSITE: Commemorative poster for the 71st Academy Awards. The concept emphasises the change of the event's day to Sunday, 1999.

SUNDAY

AT THE

OSCARS.

71ST ANNUAL ACADEMY AWARDS.

 MARCH 21,1999

Arnold Schwartzman's taste, talent, and dedication is legendary. Artist, director, designer, producer, photographer: everything he does is superlative; from making an Oscar-winning film to his dazzling and witty posters and designs for the Los Angeles Olympic Games.

— LEN DEIGHTON.

2 0 0 0

NEW YORK POST

OY VEY!

Dem big in flap over Jewish veep

Al Gore names Senator Joseph Lieberman as his Vice-Presidential running mate

Louise Nevelson (1899-1988) Jewish American sculptor honored with a set of commemorative stamps by the United States Postal Service.

1

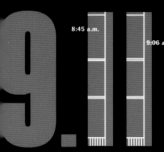

8:45 a.m. 9:06 a.m.

9.11

9/11 World Trade Center destroyed by terrorists.

American Airlines Flight 11, a Boeing 767, hijacked en route from Boston to Los Angeles with 92 passengers, crashes into the North Tower.

United Airlines Flight 175, also a Boeing 767, hijacked en route from Boston to Los Angeles with 65 passengers, crashes through the South Tower.

Mel Brooks' musical "The Producers" opens on Broadway.

2

"...I am Jewish."

The last words of Daniel Pearl, January 31, 2002

U.S. journalist Daniel Pearl executed while on assignment in Pakistan. A similar fate befell Nicholas Berg, who was murdered by terrorists in Baghdad in 2004.

"JEWCY" website and "HEEB" magazine become hip for young Jews.

Lew Wasserman, the last of Hollywood's "moguls," dies at age 89. Obituary appears on front page of the New York Times.

3

Disney Hall, designed by architect Frank Gehry

ANGELS IN AMERICA

Mike Nichols directs Tony Kushner's Broadway hit for television

Columbia Shuttle Mission patch

Mark Rothko

Architect Frank Gehry's Disney Hall opens.

Israeli astronaut Ilan Ramon killed in Columbia space shuttle disaster.

Tony Kushner adapts his epic Tony Award winning play "Angels in America" for television.

Daniel Libeskind's proposed design, "Memory Foundations," chosen for World Trade Center memorial.

Mark Rothko Centennial exhibition, Riga, Latvia and Winter Palace, St. Petersburg, Russia.

4

350

JEWISH LIFE IN AMERICA

USA

Celebrating 350 years of Jewish life in America, 1654–2004

Annie Liebovitz and Diane Arbus photographic exhibitions open in Los Angeles.

Einstein exhibition opens, co-organized by the American Museum of Natural History, New York, the Hebrew University, Jerusalem, and the Skirball Cultural Center Los Angeles.

Celebration of 350 years of Jewish life in America.

5

110

The similarity between an Oscar statuette and the image of "robot-Maria" encircled with rings of light in Fritz Lang's film *Metropolis* inspired my 2000 Academy Awards poster. The film's release in 1927 coincided with the Academy's inception.

ABOVE: Street banners, and **OPPOSITE:** Commemorative poster for the 72nd Annual Academy Awards, 2000.

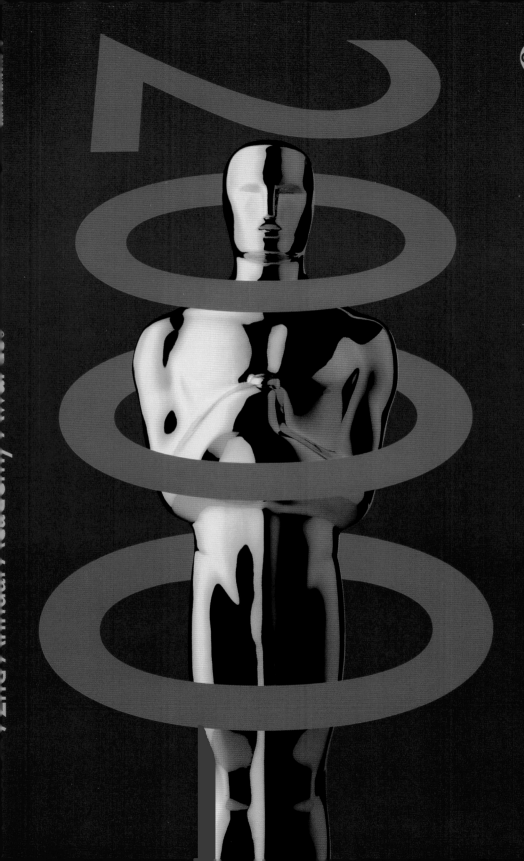

Animated neon billboard,
Sunset Boulevard, Los Angeles,
for the 72nd Annual Academy
Awards, 2000.

ABOVE: The 73rd Academy Awards Governors Ball menu cover is in the style of a turn-of-the-century "dance card", reflecting the theme of the Ball's decor, 2001.

BELOW: The 74th Academy Awards Governors Ball menu, in the style of a 1930s postcard pack, includes all previous Academy Awards presentation venues, 2002.

Photographs: John Didier, Long Photography.

ABOVE: British Academy of Film
and Television Arts/Los Angeles
Chairman Schwartzman and
Stephen Spielberg, the BAFTA/LA
2000 Britannia Award honouree.

Photograph: Alex Berliner,
Berliner Studios.

OPPOSITE: The Britannia
Award, 2002.
Sculptor: William F. Moore.
Photograph: David Peters.

*This is the heaviest award any member of the British Royal family
has been asked to present.*

– HIS ROYAL HIGHNESS THE PRINCE ANDREW, DUKE OF YORK, LOS ANGELES, 2000,
ON PRESENTING THE BRITANNIA AWARD TO STEPHEN SPIELBERG.

115

When I was asked to design a new award for
the British Academy of Film and Television
Arts/Los Angeles' annual Britannia Award,
I came up with the concept of a turned bowl,
its negative space creating a trompe l'oeil
outline of the face and helmet of "Britannia".
Each year, the awards have been crafted out
of different materials, including Cumberland
slate, oak and bronze, and titanium.

UCLA Extension

Summer Quarter begins June 23, 2001

This idea was rejected. Although Pinocchio's extended nose clearly denotes the concept of extension, it could also imply the notion of lying.

UCLA
EX$\frac{lo}{lo}$SION

Summer
Quarter
begins
June 23,
2001

118

Cover and spreads of *Flicks: How the Movies Began*, a three-dimensional book on pre-cinema history, which explores the phenomenon of the persistence of vision, incorporating many of the early cinematic devices. Each of the six spreads demonstrates the development of motion pictures. (Academy of Motion Picture Arts and Sciences, 2001). Photograph: John Didier, Long Photography.

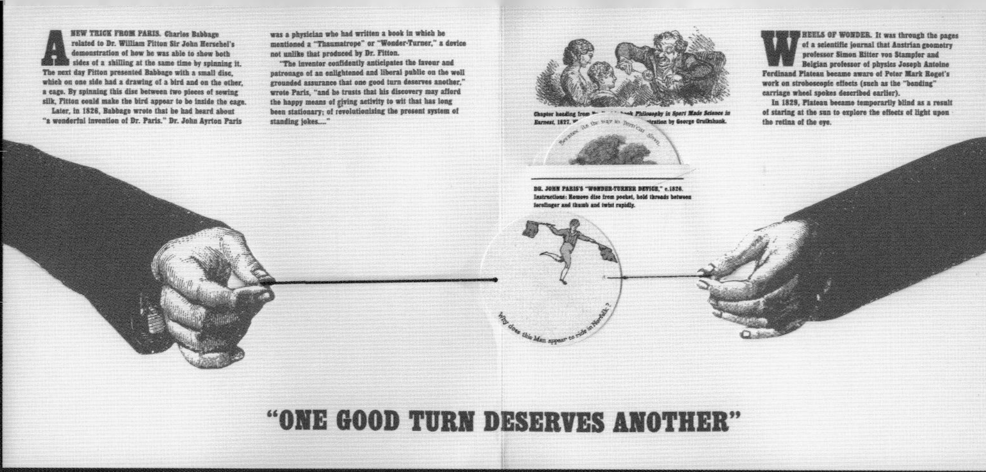

A NEW TRICK FROM PARIS. Charles Babbage related to Dr. William Fitton Sir John Herschel's demonstration of how he was able to show both sides of a shilling at the same time by spinning it. The next day Fitton presented Babbage with a small disc, which on one side had a drawing of a bird and on the other, a cage. By spinning this disc between two pieces of sewing silk, Fitton could make the bird appear to be inside the cage. Later, in 1826, Babbage wrote that he had heard about "a wonderful invention of Dr. Paris". Dr. John Ayrton Paris

was a physician who had written a book in which he mentioned a "Thaumatrope" or "Wonder-Turner," a device not unlike that produced by Dr. Fitton.

"The inventor confidently anticipates the favour and patronage of an enlightened and liberal public on the well grounded assurance that one good turn deserves another," wrote Paris, "and he trusts that his discovery may afford the happy means of giving activity to wit that has long been stationary; of revolutionizing the present system of standing jokes...."

WHEELS OF WONDER. It was through the pages of a scientific journal that Austrian geometry professor Simon Ritter von Stampfer and Belgian professor of physics Joseph Antoine Ferdinand Plateau became aware of Peter Mark Roget's work on stroboscopic effects (such as the "bending" carriage wheel spokes described earlier).

In 1829, Plateau became temporarily blind as a result of staring at the sun to explore the effects of light upon the retina of the eye.

Chapter heading from _____ Philosophy in Sport Made Science in Earnest, 1877. _____ ____tion by George Cruikshank.

DR. JOHN PARIS'S "WONDER-TURNER DEVICE," c.1826. Instructions: Remove disc from pocket, hold threads between forefinger and thumb and twist rapidly.

Why does this bird appear to ride a bicycle?

"ONE GOOD TURN DESERVES ANOTHER"

Instruction: Remove Phenakistoscope disc and handle from pocket, engage disc with tabs on handle, hold to mirror, turn disc rapidly and view images through slots.

With the assistance of his wife he continued his experiments, and around 1832 Plateau introduced his "Phenakistoscope," also known as "Phantascope," "Wheel of Wonder," and "Deceitful" or "Deceiving View."

To create the illusion of movement, the Phenakistoscope's wheel was spun before a mirror and the phase drawings were viewed through slots around the disc's edge.

Simultaneously, but independently, von Stampfer produced his "Stroboscope" or "Whirling View" disc.

(Opposite page: The Phenakistoscope)

1. REYNAUD'S PRAXINOSCOPE THÉÂTRE, 1877. 2. THÉÂTRE OPTIQUE, 1892.

ZOETROPE. William George Horner, a mathematician, conceived the "Daedalum" in 1834. The device was not patented until 1860 by Peter Desvignes, of Lewisham, England, and was later introduced to America in 1867 under the new name "Zoetrope."

(See inside back cover)

ALL DONE BY MIRRORS. The Zoetrope's invention led, in about 1877, to the perfection of the "Praxinoscope" by Frenchman Charles Émile Reynaud, a professor of natural sciences and a showman. He described his device as "photography by successive poses" or "action view." It was more sophisticated than the Zoetrope; instead of slots, it had ten mirrors mounted on a polygonal drum with sides corresponding to the number of illustrations, which revolved around a small candle or lamp mounted in the center of the drum. The Praxinoscope eliminated distortion while giving a brighter and less fatiguing image to the eye.

About 1880 Reynaud introduced a projector version of the Praxinoscope, and in 1892 opened his Théâtre Optique in Paris—the world's first movie theater—where he projected his Pantomimes Lumineuses. From a hand-coloured translucent animated strip he had the capacity of projecting more than six hundred successive images.

REYNAUD'S PROJECTION PRAXINOSCOPE, 1882.

THE HORSE IN MOTION. Edward James Muggeridge was born in Kingston upon Thames, England, in 1830. He later changed his name to Eadweard Muybridge, and proceeded to have a rather interesting life.

In the wake of the California gold rush in the early 1850s, he sailed to America and became a bookseller in San Francisco. In 1860 Muybridge was involved in a stagecoach accident in which he sustained multiple injuries, the shock turning the thirty-year-old man's hair white. Subsequently, he set himself up as a photographer.

Muybridge is most famous for his series of horse photographs, the creation of which is reputed to be the result of a bet between California Governor Leland Stanford and publisher Frederick McCrellish as to whether or not a galloping horse had, in the course of its stride, all four feet off the ground at the same time. Stanford, a racing stable owner and railway tycoon, commissioned Muybridge to take photographs of a galloping horse to prove his theory.

In October 1874, the experiment was interrupted when Muybridge learned of his wife's infidelity with a fellow Englishman. Greatly distraught, he tracked the man down and shot him dead. After much scandal, he was acquitted of the crime.

Eventually Muybridge returned to Stanford's ranch at Palo Alto, California, where, with the assistance of John Isaacs, a railway engineer in the employ of Stanford, Muybridge rigged up a battery of cameras.

EADWEARD MUYBRIDGE'S ZOOPRAXISCOPE DISC, 1882. The hand-painted figures based on Muybridge's photographs are attenuated to compensate for the distortion.

In 1878, Muybridge finally proved that a horse, in the course of its stride, momentarily has all four feet off the ground. Later that year, Muybridge filed for a patent of his "method and apparatus for photographing objects in motion." The images from his photographs were traced onto glass discs and projected by a device similar to that of Austrian Artillery officer von Uchatius's, which he called the Zoopraxiscope.

In 1881, Muybridge traveled to Europe where he was feted by the French Academy of Sciences and London's Royal Institution.

While enjoying his newfound celebrity status, Muybridge learned that Stanford had entrusted a friend, Dr. J.D.B. Stillman, with the publication of a book entitled The Horse in Motion, featuring Muybridge's photographs. Stillman neglected to credit Muybridge on the book's title page, causing him, on his return to California in 1882, to instigate legal proceedings against Stanford. In 1885, the case was settled in Stanford's favor.

Muybridge continued to photograph other animals and humans in motion. In 1894 he returned for the last time to Kingston upon Thames, where he died at age seventy-four.

THE FIRST PORTABLE CAMERA FOR PHOTOGRAPHIC MOTION, 1882. Inspired by Muybridge's work, Étienne-Jules Marey constructed the Fusil Photographique (photographic gun) in order to photograph birds in flight. Twelve exposures could be made onto a glass plate in one second by means of a clockwork and arresting mechanism.

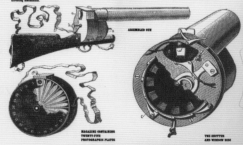

ASSEMBLED GUN

MAGAZINE CONTAINING TWENTY-FIVE PHOTOGRAPHIC PLATES

THE SHUTTER AND WINDOW DISC

MUYBRIDGE'S METHOD OF PHOTOGRAPHING A GALLOPING HORSE, c.1878. A battery of cameras was triggered by the horse's hoofs making contact with a series of trip wires.

This three-dimensional book on pre-cinema history – a personal passion – was originally produced with the prospect of being published by London's Museum of the Moving Image, but due to economic reasons the project was shelved. Fourteen years later, on showing the prototype to the president of the Academy of Motion Picture Arts and Sciences, the Academy published it under its imprint.

YOU AIN'T HEARD NOTHIN' YET... In February 1888, Thomas Alva Edison suggested to Eadweard Muybridge his idea of combining Muybridge's Zoopraxiscope with Edison's phonograph "so as to combine and reproduce simultaneously in the presence of an audience visible actions and audible words." Unfortunately, their collaboration was not to be. Over the next few decades, however, various efforts to combine sound and picture continued, until 1927, when the "talkies" became popular with the release of *The Jazz Singer*.

Between 1891 and 1893, Edison built his Black Maria film studio in West Orange, New Jersey. This tar-covered construction, built at a cost of six hundred dollars, was the world's first film studio.

Aided by his co-worker, William Kennedy Laurie Dickson, Edison's first film was of his assistant, Fred Ott, sneezing.

INTERMITTENT MOVEMENT enables a frame of film to be held still in the gate during projection and then momentarily shuttered off (so the screen is dark) while the next frame is advanced.

THOMAS EDISON'S KINETOSCOPE, 1893. A viewing cabinet, which used perforated photographic celluloid film.

In 1894, Edison introduced commercially his "Kinetoscope," or "Moving View Peepshow." This device, which could only be viewed by one person at a time, became most popular in Kinetoscope Parlors, which were opened in New York, Paris and London. Presenting forty-six frames per second, the Kinetoscope used a band of 35mm film which contained twelve hundred individual frames. The 35mm film gauge remains the standard to the present day.

CASLER'S MUTOSCOPE, 1894, later became known as "What the butler saw."

SEEING IS BELIEVING. In 1894, two French chemists and brothers named Louis Jean and August Marie Lumière saw Thomas Edison's Kinetoscope at an arcade in Paris. They set out to change the viewing of moving pictures from a single person experience to a group activity. By adapting the mechanism of a sewing machine, the brothers Lumière produced a machine that not only projected film, but could expose it as well. They patented their process on February 13, 1895.

And so, on December 28, 1895, Louis and Auguste Lumière premiered their Cinematographe in the Grand Cafe, Paris—the world's first public screening of motion pictures. Their first program included *Dinner Hour at the Factory Gate of M. Lumière at Lyons*, *The Blacksmith at Work*, and *A Practical Joke in the Garden*. Admission was one franc.

The brothers, whose motto was "catch nature in the act," did not regard themselves as showmen, but looked upon their invention as a scientific achievement.

GRASPING AT SHADOWS. Many contributed to the advent of the movies. One of those, a French photographer, Louis Aimé Augustin Le Prince, of Leeds, England, having solved most of the essentials necessary for filming and projecting motion pictures in 1888—some seven years before the Lumière brothers—boarded a train in Dijon for Paris on September 16, 1890. He, his luggage and apparatus vanished without a trace. The investigating police could find no clues, a mystery that remains unsolved to this day.

Other pioneers who contributed to the development of the cinema were: the Langenheim brothers (Hyalotype, c.1849), Franz von Uchatius (Heliocinegraph, 1853), Coleman Sellers (Kinematoscope, c.1861), John Beale (Choreutoscope, c.1866), John A. Roebuck Rudge (Bio-Phantascope, c.1866), Reverend Hannibal Goodwin (celluloid film, 1877),

THE LUMIÈRE BROTHERS' CINÉMATOGRAPHE, 1895.

ZOETROPE STRIP

Ottomar Anschütz (Tachyscope, 1887), George Eastman (celluloid film, 1889), William Friese-Greene (film camera, c.1889), Georges Démeny (Phonoscope, c.1892), Max Sklafanowsky (Bioscope, 1895), W. Latham (Eidoloscope, 1895), Birt Acres (Cinematoscope, 1895), Robert W. Paul (Animatograph, 1896), the Isola brothers (Isolatograph, c.1896), Oskar Messter (Maltese Cross, c.1896), Thomas Armat (Vitascope, 1896), Armat and C. Francis Jenkins (Phantascope, 1894).

There were many disputes and legal battles, particularly those between Muybridge and Stanford, Armat and Jenkins, Dickson and Edison, and Eastman and the Reverend Goodwin. One disputant proclaimed that the cinema was an invention of an epoch, rather than an individual.

The toy had now come of age, and the pioneers of the cinema had turned the silver screen into a gold rush.

ACKNOWLEDGEMENTS: Grateful thanks to John Barnes; Bethnal Green Museum of Childhood, London; British Film Institute; Ben Barrows; Len Beighton; David Francis; Colin W. Harding; Kingston upon Thames Museum and Art Gallery; Margaret Herrick Library; David Pollard; Tony Usman; Science Museum, London; Inside Schwartzman; Universal Studios Archives and Collections.

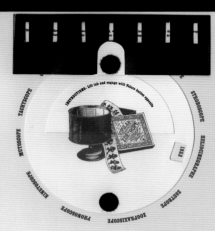

INSTRUCTIONS: lift tab and engage with Velcro button system

TACHYSCOPE · STROBOSCOPE · HELIOCINEGRAPH · 1863 · ZONTROPE · ZOOPRAXISCOPE · PHONOSCOPE · KINETOSCOPE · MUTOSCOPE

A "scrapbook" of film-related ephemera from the Academy's Margaret Herrick Library, celebrating the 75th Academy Awards Governors Ball, 2003.

LIBERATION

PacificDesignCenter

Logotypes:
1: Four semi-circles create the name "Duda", for Duda Design.

2: Documentary film *Liberation*, Morse code spells "V for Victory".
3: An architect's scale represents the Pacific Design Center.

4: "Oscars" for an exhibition of Schwartzman's designs for the Academy Awards, 2000.

1: Symbol for the 60th anniversary of *The King of Lampedusa* – a play based on the true story of a Royal Air Force pilot in WWII.
2: Symbol for the exhibition *Folk Art from A to Z.*

3: Logo for Creative Talent Communications, a public relations company. Masks of Tragedy and Comedy are formed out of the letters C and T.

4: Symbol for Limelight, a film production company.
5: Logo for the Jewish Image Awards. The interwoven letter form a menorah (ceremonial candelabra).

A spread and cover from
*DECO LAndmarks:
Art Deco Gems of Los Angeles.*
(Chronicle Books, 2005)

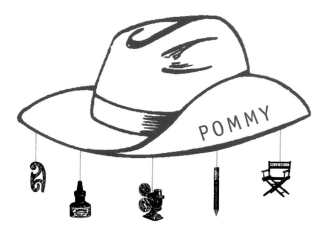

Arnie made his life and work seem very reasonable. A seamless progression of a life; which is disconcerting because this 'grand statesman of design' is indeed very talented and forever seeking and living his work.

Arnie talked of his work as a gradual evolution of interest, opportunities and coincidences giving a human dimension to his work. His generosity of spirit showed and glowed through. One could expect him to be a great teacher, and he did talk of his perception of the ennui in contemporary design education.

— *AMPERSAND*, REPORT ON SCHWARTZMAN'S TALK TO THE AUSTRALIAN GRAPHIC DESIGNERS ASSOCIATION AT THE NATIONAL PRESS CLUB, CANBERRA, AUSTRALIA, MAY 1998.

ABOVE: Symbol for Schwartzman's lecture tour of Australia, 1998.

BELOW: A fan depicting a satellite view of the Great Wall of China for a themed project and exhibition for the Alliance

Graphique Internationale Congress held in Beijing, Republic of China, 2004.

Arnold Schwartzman, O.B.E.

1936 Born Wapping, London, England

1951–52 Thanet School of Art and Crafts, Kent

1953–55 Canterbury College of Art, Kent

1955–57 Military service, Germany and Korea

1959 Graphic designer, Southern Television

1959–66 Graphic designer,
Associated-Rediffusion Television

1966 Concept planning executive,
Erwin Wasey Advertising

1969 Graphics Director/Member of the Board,
Conran Design Group

1970 Formed Arnold Schwartzman Productions,
Design and Film consultancy

1965–1978 A regular illustrator for
The Sunday Times, Man About Town,
Radio Times, New Society, Queen and Vogue

1970 Designed The Sunday Times Magazine
supplement Eureka: A History of Inventions

1974 Designed The Sunday Times Magazine
supplement The Facts of Life:
Man's Discovery of Himself

1978 Design Director,
Paul Bass and Associates, Los Angeles

1982 Appointed the Director of Design for
the 1984 Los Angeles Olympic Games

1993 Produced a number of graphic and
video exhibits for the Museum of Tolerance

1996 Created a permanent eight-screen
video exhibit, a "Time Line" mural, plus several
short films, for the Skirball Cultural Center

Documentary Feature Films:

Producer/Director: Genocide, 1981,
Academy Award winner

Producer/Director: Building A Dream:
The story of the 1932 Los Angeles Olympic Games,
1989

Producer/director: Echoes That Remain, 1991

Producer/director: Liberation, 1994

Books:

Airshipwreck with Len Deighton
(Jonathan Cape, 1978)

Graven Images: Graphic Motifs of the
Jewish Gravestone (Harry N. Abrams, 1993)

Phono-Graphics: The Visual Paraphernalia of
the Talking Machine (Chronicle Books, 1993)

Liberation (Companion to documentary film)
(Museum of Tolerance, 1994)

Designage: The Art of the Decorative Sign
(Chronicle Books, 1998)

It's a Great Wall, with Michael Webb
(The Images Publishing Group, 2000)

Flicks: How The Movies Began (Academy of Motion
Picture Arts and Sciences, 2001)

DECO LAndmarks: Art Deco Gems of Los Angeles.
(Chronicle Books, 2005)

Outside Activities:

Governor and past Chairman of the British
Academy of Film and Television Arts Los Angeles
(BAFTA/LA); past Chairman of the
Documentary Executive Committee of the
Academy of Motion Picture Arts and Sciences;
member of the National Foundation for Jewish
Culture's Los Angeles Entertainment Industry
Council; the Board of Hollywood Heritage, Inc.;
and the Board of Trustees of the
Craft and Folk Art Museum

Awards:

Recipient of an Oscar and other film awards, as
well as a number of international design awards,
including three Designers and Art Directors
Association of London Silver awards

1974 Elected to the
Alliance Graphique Internationale

2000 Received the Pacific Design Center's
Stars of Design Life Achievement Award
for Graphic Design.

2002 Appointed an Officer of the Order of
the British Empire (O.B.E.) in Her Majesty
The Queen's New Year's Honours List for
services to the British film industry in the U.S.A.

**OVERLEAF: Poster announcing the
International Design Masters
Forum, Shanghai, Republic of
China, 2004.**

127